PTOXOCRACY

Ptoxocracy

An End to Christianity

M. C. LOHRMANN

WIPF & STOCK · Eugene, Oregon

PTOXOCRACY
An End to Christianity

Copyright © 2025 M. C. Lohrmann. All rights reserved. Except for brief quotations in critical publications or reviews, no part of this book may be reproduced in any manner without prior written permission from the publisher. Write: Permissions, Wipf and Stock Publishers, 199 W. 8th Ave., Suite 3, Eugene, OR 97401.

Wipf & Stock
An Imprint of Wipf and Stock Publishers
199 W. 8th Ave., Suite 3
Eugene, OR 97401

www.wipfandstock.com

PAPERBACK ISBN: 979-8-3852-4000-5
HARDCOVER ISBN: 979-8-3852-4001-2
EBOOK ISBN: 979-8-3852-4002-9

VERSION NUMBER 05/19/25

Unless noted otherwise, all Scripture quotations are taken from the New Revised Standard Version Updated Edition. Copyright © 2021 National Council of Churches of Christ in the United States of America. Used by permission. All rights reserved worldwide.

*To Elijah, Isaak, and Bekki,
delights of my heart.*

ptoxocracy
(p·toeks·*AW*·kruh·see)

governance by the *ptoxoi*; a hybrid form of representative democracy whereby only persons of the lowest economic status are eligible for elected public office

Contents

Preface | ix

Acknowledgments | xi

Introduction: The Treasures of the Church | 1

1   The Poor Are Always Forgotten | 14

2   The Mythology of the Rich Ruling Class | 38

3   Ptoxocracy | 56

4   Interrogating Ptoxocracy | 74

5   Blessed Are the *Ptoxoi* | 98

6   Ptoxocracy and the Church | 119

7   The Ptoxocratic Lens | 138

Conclusion: An End to Christianity | 157

Bibliography | 167

Preface

THE NOTION OF PTOXOCRACY first arose in my mind during the final descent into a municipal airport on my way to a family reunion. I had never been to the area, but I marveled at the dense forests of deciduous trees below swathed in what I would quickly come to find was a thick humidity. As the plane drew low enough to make out the shapes below, I noticed that the landscape was dotted with what appeared to be a mixture of mining operations and farmlands. It reminded me of the similar mixture of industrial farms, rugged topography, and family homesteads in eastern Washington State, where I was raised. I couldn't help but wonder how many of those mines or industrial complexes were owned by homeowners or community members nearby that we were passing over, and what share these citizens might have had in the benefits of these industrial forces. If it was anything like my homelands, much of the industrial capital would be owned by persons who were not immediate neighbors, while many of the negative consequence of these forces would be felt locally. Generations of animosity felt during childhood between the rich on one side of Washington State and us in eastern Washington flooded back to me and struck me for the first time as deeply plutocratic in nature. I chuckled to myself as I parsed a word that conveyed the opposite to plutocracy, reaching into my divinity-school biblical-Greek memory bank to do so: *ptoxocracy*. I had never heard that word before.

The idea of ptoxocracy that took root during that final descent in late July 2023 continued to pester me until I first outlined my ideas in a journal that autumn. Completing a first draft in December that year, I set the manuscript down until midsummer, whereupon I set about revising and reshaping the ideas considerably before sharing it with some trusted friends. If the word didn't exist, the aims of that early project were to articulate why not, and how the word might function if taken seriously.

PREFACE

Upon receiving a formal offer to publish from Wipf & Stock that August, I began another wholehearted revision of the project, taking the early readers' feedback seriously enough to turn it upside down entirely once again.

It has become newly pertinent to write about the troubling relationship between power and wealth, and the ways that faith calls us to question the givenness of this seemingly foregone conclusion, as evidenced in the collective net worth of the United States cabinet at the time of publishing. In these days of strange political upheaval at the hands of wealth that defies both imagination and scope, this project has become both life giving and exhausting at once. The political landscape has both weighed on me and urged me toward completion, just as the magnetism of wealth and political power has become devastatingly clearer with each day.

Songwriter Jeff Tweedy wrote in his 2018 memoir that the highest purpose of all works of art is "to inspire someone else to save themselves through art. Creating creates creators."[1] Preachers, like songwriters, are artists whose works attempt to create creators among listeners. If the first aim of this project was to articulate a vision of ptoxocracy from scratch, the latest version has yielded another, to provoke others to poke, prod, analyze, and criticize ptoxocracy, with the explicit goal of bettering the lives of poor persons and, by extension, everyone else. My sincere hope is to "create creators" who might become partners toward this end.

MARCUS CHRISTIAN LOHRMANN
CALIFORNIA, MARCH 2025

---

1. Tweedy, *Let's Go*, 74.

Acknowledgments

When I first let my congregation's leaders know that I had been composing what would become *Ptoxocracy: An End to Christianity*, I did so in request of a two-week break from my pastoral duties to work alongside my editor toward completion of the final manuscript. One of the board members, Patricia, piped up and teased me, "You can have your two weeks so long as you thank us in the acknowledgment section."

"I hadn't thought of that, Pat," I winked, "but I suppose you've got yourself a deal."

Loving jokes aside, this book would not have been written but for the opportunity to serve Shepherd of the Valley Lutheran Church in La Mesa, California, for which I am sincerely grateful. You were at the top of the acknowledgments section all along, Pat. For the curious hearts of our Bible study groups, council members, worshipping members, and more, folks who invigorate and inform this work in more ways than you know, thank you. To Antoine, Ron, Tanya, Deb, Eldon, Gina, and the many others with whom I am so fortunate to work alongside in this place: thank you. For the church members who graciously support me in not only this work, but all my pastoral endeavors, thank you. I also want to thank our neighbors at St. Peter's by the Sea Lutheran Church in San Diego for the generous use of a workspace during those intensive weeks of writing and editing. I suspect that an uninterrupted view of the Pacific Ocean is nearly every writer's dream, and you have made mine come true.

Benjamin Bahr was the earliest conversation partner on ptoxocracy. Thank you, Ben, for the many rounds of conversation through which you seriously engaged the many problems and implications of the ideas at hand, as well as your constant encouragement during every step of the way. I also want to thank Paul Palumbo who, alongside Ben, graciously read the first draft of *Ptoxocracy* in full and provided important insights that profoundly

ACKNOWLEDGMENTS

shaped its final inception. There is nothing so refreshing as the clear-eyed honesty of good companions who are unafraid to tell you what they really think when something isn't working, and these two were truly great. Toward that end, an enormous word of thanks to my editor, Nancy Bryan, without whose sure-footed guidance, trusted companionship, and wisdom this project would never have come to completion.

Those teachers who inspired me toward this endeavor over the years are far too many to name. Among these, Cynthia Lindner sent me off into the world as a young pastor many years ago and continues to surprise me in returning my phone calls and showing up for loving conversations when I most need counsel, usually around delicious food. True to form, she was happy to engage this project in an important moment of need, and helped embolden me toward the finish line amid a period of deep uncertainty. Thank you for the ways you support and love your students, Cynthia, even when we're no longer enrolled in the ministry program.

To my parents, John and Linda, who helped see my family through the seasons between Advent and Lent 2024–2025, never complaining about the extra hours spent playing with my kids as I holed up to work on this book: thank you. I suspect you enjoyed the time as much as the kids did, but I am grateful, nevertheless. Thanks, also, for being people whose faith encourages personal growth, curiosity, and trust.

Finally, to my children Elijah and Isaak, thank you for your patience, smiles, and tender hearts, and to my best friend and partner, Bekki. People often ask me what it's like to be married to another Lutheran pastor. While it means that our eldest child regularly reminds us of our family's "no church-talk at the dinner table" rule, it also means that I get to live with the best theologian and pastor I know. This undoubtedly makes for better preaching and pastoring on my part, and it means I am also granted an exceptional partner in a shared journey of parenting, marriage, and vocation. Much like Ben, Bekki's early investigation and conversations around ptoxocracy were fundamental. She served as my clearness committee in important times of uncertainty, pushed me to deepen my ideas where they were vague or ambiguous, and enriched the project with her own theological insights over many conversations. This book would not have been written without Bekki's encouragement, support, and love at every step of the way, for which I am profoundly grateful.

MARCUS CHRISTIAN LOHRMANN
CALIFORNIA, MARCH 2025

Introduction

The Treasures of the Church

THERE'S A STORY ABOUT a saint of the third-century Jesus movement named Lawrence, deacon of Rome. The city of Rome faced a financial crisis, and the city's prefect hauled Lawrence before him citing evidence that the church was hoarding treasure that belonged to the state. The prefect had been hearing rumors among his spies that the followers of Jesus spoke often and loudly of the *treasures of the church*, and felt convinced that Lawrence, into whose care the treasury had been given, must be behind the conspiracy to hide these. As beckoned, Lawrence came and stood before the prefect, who demanded that he cede this treasure to the city's treasury at once.

Lawrence scratched his head. While it was true that he had been set in charge of the church's meager funds, he and his coworkers had no stashes of hidden gold or diamonds. The more the city leader ordered him to surrender this treasure, the more confused he became. Suddenly an idea came to him. He assented to the prefect and asked for three days' time to collect this treasure. Some versions of the legend say that Lawrence and a coworker spent those days donating what few monetary goods the church had to the poor. (At this point of the story, one either must believe Lawrence was a sweet and innocent deacon or a clever political adversary of the prefect. Since the line between church history and church legend is blurry, I tend to prefer the former because it makes children's sermons on this story more fun to tell.)

Three days later and full of excitement, Lawrence bounded into the prefect's court. All manner of sick, wounded, despondent, materially poor, and houseless persons came in beside him. The court took on an odor unpleasant to the prefect, who was now predictably agitated at the offense of these poor and destitute huddled inside his court. "Here they are,"

Lawrence said with excitement, pointing at those gathered in the prefect's quarters, "the treasures of the church!"

The authorities of Rome had little interest in the church's treasure, and Lawrence was sentenced to death on a gridiron and coals. The early church, in contrast to Rome and its prefect, understood that the most authentic expression of itself was not in accumulation of goods or political power, but in care of the marginalized. These were her riches: the destitute, the homeless, the widow, the orphan, the sick, the dying, and the abject poor, and she clung to them. Like Lawrence, on account of this authentic expression of herself, the church would suffer persecution.

As their own story continued to be written, the Christian faithful would undergo a centuries-long metamorphosis of integration into the Roman state. In the introduction of his massive work *The New Roman Empire: A History of Byzantium*, historian Anthony Kaldellis notes that, whereas Christian apologists tend to make triumphal claims about their religion over that of pagan Roman religions, Christianity's adoption in the fourth century as the state-sanctioned faith of the empire changed little about day-to-day life within its boundaries. He writes that "macroscopically, the empire's conversion [to Christianity] changed virtually nothing in the economy, social and political structure, army, tax practices, and political history of the Roman empire."[1] Yet, he notes, the church itself changed drastically. In assimilating Roman governmental structures into its own church structure, the Christian church took on a form that often could be more aptly mistaken for the court of this nameless Roman prefect than of Lawrence. "It is not clear," writes Kaldellis, "whether Christianity 'triumphed' over the Roman order or was captured by it."[2]

There is a sense within the church today, an unsettled feeling that broods around the edges of every conversation, space of worship, and meeting, that something in Christianity is deeply wrong, especially as it relates to, and exists within, the wider world of systems that harbor suspicions of the church's most authentic treasures. The church has confused her true treasures for those of the prefect, exchanging care of the poor and destitute for political power and wealth.

John of Patmos, writer of the book of Revelation, seems to have had a similar idea as he composed his own work at an earlier historical juncture. Peering into a landscape riddled with division and antagonism between

---

1. Kaldellis, *New Roman Empire*, 62.
2. Kaldellis, *New Roman Empire*, 62.

INTRODUCTION

Christians, and with the Roman war machine injecting brutality into the everyday lives of citizens, John of Patmos peered across the horizon toward a vision of hope beyond the seeming end of all things, of a hope beyond that despair. Biblical scholar Barbara Rossing urges readers to interpret his work as "a timely warning, not a prediction." She writes, "[John of Patmos's] apocalypse spoke a daring word, pulling back the curtain to expose Rome's brutality and illegitimacy."[3] He sensed the temptation that Rome, wise in its capacity to lure followers with promises of political domination, might bring the church to ruin, and issued warnings accordingly of her temptation.

To read Revelation literally—that is, to read it as a script of some apocalyptic future which God is beholden to follow—misses the thrust of John's project entirely. Rossing encourages readers, rather, to interpret Revelation in much the same way that readers enjoy Charles Dickens's *A Christmas Carol*. In that story, Scrooge, the main character, is famously visited by three ghosts: the past, present, and future. The first two ghosts show the world, as well as his position within it, accurately. He sees with harsh clarity his life as it has been lived, and as it is presently. The trajectory of this life seems to be the lonesome death of a miser, yet in the end he receives the gift of an alternative future: although the ghosts of past and present remain true, he has the capacity to shape his reality toward the good. The ghost of Christmas future presents a vision of what may be, not a vision of what must be. The same is true of Revelation. The same will be, I hope, true of this book.

Christianity does not have to be a religion of patriarchy, political domination, sexism, gender conformity, rigidity, or violence, yet we find troubling traces of these dynamics within Christian communities and practices worldwide today in its manifold institutional expressions, both formal and informal. We hear these as the howls of ghosts of present and past resonating through a complex history of Christianity's relationship with empire, but we are at an impasse: it's not too late for followers of Jesus to make drastic alterations to our course. The future is yet ours to build as we wish, and the invitation to exchange our present treasures of wealth and political power for the true treasures of the church is still at hand.

Before being ordained as a Lutheran pastor, I worked in the wine industry in the greater Chicago area. Trying to keep the bills paid so that I could pursue my songwriting habit in earnest by night, I worked in a

3. Rossing, *Rapture Exposed*, 87.

midsized restaurant and retail space that specialized in farm-to-table dining, artisanal cheeses, and small batch beer, wine, and spirits. It was a great place to meet other young, excited artists and aspiring talent whose day jobs there also paid the bills in service of their passions. I met interns with local public radio stations supporting their internships as bartenders, cheesemongers hustling as graphic designers on the side, and playwrights paying the bills as restaurant managers for a chance to break into the extensive nonprofit theatre scene in Chicago. Though it was situated in a midwestern suburb, the kind of place you might expect to be filled with stalwart, mainline-denominational churchgoers in another age, almost none of the fifty-plus folks I worked alongside in that business identified as people of the Christian faith. In fact, as I came to understand over the next few years, while most of the people I'd work beside had grown up in the church, most had left the churches of their childhood, and readily articulated a palpable sense of relief and freedom in pursuit of their own meaning-making communities outside of it. Some of these were ambivalent, but others expressed open fury at organized religion's hypocrisy. It wasn't just that church wasn't cool, it was that the church itself as an institution seemed an obstacle to living the kind of meaningful lives that they were pursuing in their endeavors as artists, entrepreneurs, or simply as workers who needed to pay the bills. To these people who cared about the environment, social justice movements, the well-being of the poor, art, self-expression, and even democracy, the church appeared an antagonist to be overcome rather than an ally to be cherished.

This book is partly written for those individuals I used to work alongside; their constant frustration with the church as a source of meaning and good continues to break my heart, in part for them, but in part for what the church is missing out on from them. This book is also written for the people of today's church who feel a similar call to attend to and exist within the world as we find it, yet who, because of civil and church structures, traditions, class, social norms, or any other barriers, do not find within the church that call of solidarity with the poor beyond charity, but who faithfully stay nevertheless. What I heard from my fellow hourly-wage workers years ago, often now categorized as religious *nones*, was a troubling refrain: that if the church really cared about the poor and disenfranchised, why couldn't it get off its high horse and do something meaningful? The disconnect between value and action was perceived as inauthenticity. In other words, I heard a real frustration with the incapacity of Christian

INTRODUCTION

communities to go beyond mere lip service to the center of what seemed so important to the person of Jesus—namely, what Lawrence knew to be the center: the poor.

Lawrence understood the center of Christ's ministry well enough to lay down his own body for it, and my sense is that Christians today do as well, even if we can't always figure out how to do this ourselves. Now that I serve as a pastor within a North American context—an ordained minister who only occasionally regrets leaving the wine industry—I continue to engage with countless well-meaning persons of faith whose dissatisfaction with the reality of poverty is palpable. Some of these have left already, and some still hold out hope that the church can find its way. Where previous generations may have felt a similar dissatisfaction but stayed in the church, today people are free to vote with their feet. It's no accident that the average age of my congregation is in their late sixties, as many of those out the door have tended to be younger. To philosopher Charles Taylor's point, life in a secular age means that for the first time in recent human history, simply leaving the church is an option.[4] Leaving church is a viable expression of frustration, one that was less acceptable for persons of other generations. It's a new phenomenon, one that I am afraid to say still surprises some of my pastoral colleagues. Church membership is on the decline, and instead of accepting this, I constantly hear pastors express anger, frustration, and disdain for religious *nones*, rather than asking hard questions of themselves and the institutions we serve.

The church's typical response to the poor is charity, yet what I have come to recognize in pastoral ministry is that charity has clear limitations. This is, I understand, an ironic argument to make as a person whose salary is paid in large part by the generosity of tax-deductible donations received by my organization as charity. It does explain, however, one of the reasons that religious leaders may find themselves in such an uncomfortable position: critiquing the system that inadequately addresses poverty has clear ramifications for our livelihoods and is a dangerous enterprise existentially. Self-interest quiets these concerns because pastors, like any other citizen, must also pay their bills. Yet systems matter, and charity, as a system, comes up short. Think of the ways that we hear people speak about charitable organizations and the *effective* or *successful use* of each dollar donated, the myriads of analytical frameworks devised to sell one charity over another as *more* effective. Martin Luther King Jr., whom we often forget served as

---

4. Taylor, *Secular Age*, 3.

a pastor, also knew the limits of charity. Liz Theoharis, cochair of the Poor People's Campaign and scholar of ethics around issues of poverty, sums the problem with charity up nicely. She and coauthor Colleen Wessel-McCoy write that "ideologically, charity functions to demonstrate how much the rich care about the poor."[5] This is exactly the kind of criticism of the church that I heard from my old coworkers. Theoharis and Wessel-McCoy go on: "Through this system the rich of the world are able to hide the reality—that the necessary cause and consequence of their wealth is the impoverishment of the poor—behind the ideology that they and their wealth are actually the saviors of the poor and common people."[6] Charity fails the heart of Christianity because at its core is not the well-being of the poor, but the rich. It is a piecemeal solution to a systemic reality, one whose primary, though not sole beneficiary, is the rich. Lawrence didn't get a tax write-off for his good deeds caring for homeless and sick; his deeds grew out of fidelity and faith to the Gospel of Jesus.

The aim of this book is to fashion a system toward the well-being of the poor. We may also discover that in attending to the poor, we will also better attend to the spiritual lives of the rich. These do not need to be mutually exclusive goals, as is often portrayed. Kaldellis, again as a historian, notes that there are indeed other faith traditions whose structures of governance follow from the ethical implications of theological commitments, and whose own structures then flow into and influence the structures of civil society. As a primary example, Kaldellis cites Islam as one form of civil governance structure which flows naturally from theological commitments, rather than receiving these from the outside. In contrast to Islam, Kaldellis argues, Christianity's adoption by Roman authority meant that any efforts of its own to develop an organic governmental structure out of its theological commitments were stymied before they could get started. By contrast, the state and religious organizations of Islam are intimately intertwined and mutually informed. Christianity as an institution structured itself as a mirror to the old governmental Roman order set on top of it. Its theological commitments, in other words, took a back seat to Roman civil order. Even those ecclesial bodies like mine who broke formally from Roman mechanisms continue to organize with hierarchies of authorities, committees, budgets, and constitutions that do more to echo Roman civil society than they do, say, Jesus's Sermon on the Mount. Today's church,

---

5. Theoharis and Wessel-McCoy, "More than Flinging a Coin," para. 9.
6. Theoharis and Wessel-McCoy, "More than Flinging a Coin," para. 9.

both in its local and wider expressions, functions essentially as a collective of small democratic pockets whose organizational structures mirror civic organizations, not unlike other nonprofit organizations. What this means, then, is that the structural authority and organization of the church itself is confined and committed to non-Christian structural realities *before* it arrives at theological commitments. There becomes only limited opportunity to imagine a system of governing structure that is, for example, deeply informed by the Sermon on the Mount, whose structural order might very well prioritize peacemaking or compassion before it prioritizes order. There is, in other words, no imagination given to a native structure of government in which one might "turn the other cheek" when it comes to a system of jurisprudence and retributive justice, no formalized and developing system in which love of enemies is prioritized as the highest possible good of national identity and diplomatic ends.

Following Kaldellis, we can argue that the opposite occurred, that Rome's adoption of Christianity subsumed it in a culture that smacks directly in opposition to the teachings of Jesus. Howard Thurman argues in his monumental *Jesus and the Disinherited* that the historical man we know as Jesus of Nazareth lived a contextual life in direct opposition and daily confrontation with these very structures, forces, and systems of Roman authority, and that to ignore Jesus's embodied reality as son of Mary and Joseph is to ignore much of the important implications of his teachings. Mary and Joseph were refugees forced to flee at the hands of a murderous head-of-state, Jesus was a Jew (and not just any Jew but one whose devotion to his locale and its values is an invaluable interpretive lens when we examine the nature of his ministry and mission), and further, Jesus was a *poor* Jew. Thurman writes, "The economic predicament with which he was identified in birth placed him initially with the great mass of men on the earth. The masses of the people. Our poor."[7] How can we expect the church to function authentically toward the poor if, in its bones, it simply mirrors the structural commitments of a wealthy empire, the one which, in fact, put him to death? How can the church hope to begin the task of reclaiming Lawrence's treasures if we constantly choose to orient ourselves by way of the treasures of the prefect? The Roman adoption of Christianity completely disrupts and short-circuits its theological commitments, leaving them as mere moral imperatives whose ideals are high but whose political implications are unserious at best. In effect, the church, having

---

7. Thurman, *Jesus and the Disinherited*, 7.

adopted these civic structures, has become infected with systems that are non-native to its own ideals.

Theocracy—that is, government by the theologically trained—is not the answer to this problem, nor is it a solution indigenous to the Christian biblical imagination. It's important, since we're speaking here of religion, political power, and society, to outrightly reject theocracy as a viable form of civil government indigenous to the Christian tradition. Nothing in the ministry of Jesus suggests that his aims were earthly political power and wealth. Quite the contrary.

While it deals with structures of political power, this book is ultimately a work of constructive theology. I write from the perspective of a pastor who lives and works in the tension between systems that claim to prioritize the needs of the poor, yet whose designs and structures lend themselves to both accommodation of and subjection to de facto rule by the rich. How might we take the Sermon on the Mount (or the Plain) seriously enough to question our structures of governance, even if these questions endanger the very livelihood that give whatever small authority it can muster to this argument itself? Others, particularly here I'm thinking of those within the Anabaptist tradition, have undertaken similar projects, and I recognize that mine is merely one attempt among many in a long line of those who have raised a similar problem of Christian dissonance with the political structures of our world. The ugly history of early Lutheran theological, political, and physical dominance over precisely these traditions leads me not only to acknowledge these, but to proceed humbly as good-faith partner in the aim of furthering the mission of God together alongside their work. While this book will not explicitly deal in analyzing or replicating these works, the work of undoing a violent history between Lutherans and Anabaptists (that is, the former's historical and violent domination of the latter) continues here by way of acknowledgment, gratitude, and humility.

For those readers who are either uncomfortable or unfamiliar with the genre of constructive theology, we can easily look back to Dickens's *Christmas Carol* for help. Scrooge sees a vision of past and present, and these visions trouble him. Yet the time for change is still ripe, and Scrooge's vision of the future need not actually happen. What he needs is a chance to lean into a new vision of life, a way forward that acknowledges the past, but holds fast to that which was once unthinkable. This is constructive theology. What follows is a vision, one which arises out of scriptural, philosophical, and theological ideas, for the future of a church who truly attends to the poor, a church that treasures them as deeply as Lawrence, and thereby attends to the well-being of all others in society.

The goal of this book, then, is to articulate what sociologist and theologian Hans Joas terms a "possible future" for the church, toward which the church could aim if it so desired.[8] It is a possible future that is both perfectly feasible (in the sense that it doesn't require divine intervention, even if it seems implausible under the weight of history) and aligns with values inherent to Christian theology. This is the *end of Christianity* which this book articulates. Admittedly, there is a second sense in which I mean an *end* to Christianity, that such a future would indeed spell the end to Christianity as we have come to inherit it. I expect this to be a much less comfortable, and no less radical idea. Again, it's a difficult pill to swallow for anyone whose paychecks come from a church, like me.

Dickens's ghosts change the course of Scrooge's life and lead him into an altered future that would not have occurred without warning. This text, similarly, also comes with a warning: should institutional Christianity continue to decenter the concerns of the poor, the heart of both the ancient prophets concern as well as the historical Jesus's, it is likely to continue in a trajectory toward institutional demise. Nothing about this statement, though audacious, should surprise us. Given all we have heard from actual social scientists about current trends in organized religion in North America, it's hardly even radical. The prophets of the Hebrew Bible—Amos, Jeremiah, and Isaiah—all follow similar patterns of concern, which can be paraphrased as, "Tread the poor down for the sake of the rich, and you can definitely expect the worst to happen." Warnings and precaution are not faithless; they are expressions of hope amid the clamor of despair, as timeless as the prophet Amos's warning to God's people millennia ago. Empirical evidence demonstrates this decline today, and the work of theologians, philosophers, sociologists, and social scientists demonstrates this work to a higher degree than I intend to do here. Charles Taylor, the Pew Research Center, Phyllis Tickle, Richard Rohr, Diana Butler Bass, nearly every parish pastor I know, and a host of others come to mind. Revisions and renewals to church worship, administrative practices, liturgy, governance, and the like will continue as fruitless endeavors unless the institution centers and reclaims its attention to the poor and looks beyond charity in its aim to do so.

---

8. Joas, *Faith as an Option*, 116–25.

Amos, pronouncing God's warning to the people, writes, "I hate, I despise your festivals, and I take no delight in your solemn assemblies" (Amos 5:21). God's warning of wrath emerges for many reasons, but chief among them is the failure of the religious institutions of his people to center the concerns and well-being of the poor, the widow, the orphan, and the foreigner. God's wrath is upon the people precisely "*because* you trample on the poor and take from them levies of grain" (5:11a, emphasis added). The words of the prophet are not unlike Scrooge's vision, and not unlike the aims of what follows. It may be possible to avert exile in the unknown lands of denominational decline, but the pathway of life for the church will be through the poor, not around them. Anecdotally, my observation is that before the pandemic, most faith leaders were anxious about this decline. Post-pandemic, however, anxiety has turned to despair. Again, the aim of this book is simple: to articulate a possible and realistic future for the church beyond exactly this despair. In this, it is a project indigenous to the tradition insofar as it resists death itself as the final word.

A few words of orientation as we begin. First, as the reader has probably already noticed, I will use the terms *rich* and *poor* frequently in this text. I employ these terms in the tradition of great theologians like Martin Luther King Jr., Gustavo Gutiérrez, and Howard Thurman, whose work has deeply shaped this project. I am, moreover, a person located within the category of the rich. As a land-owning Californian, I tend to self-identify as middle class. Yet relative to other human beings on this planet, I am absolutely among the rich, and I do not mean this in a spiritual sense. For this reason, and others, I can comfortably call myself rich in this project and count myself among that number.

Further, any time I use the words *rich* or *poor* I will attempt to do so without a hint of condemnation, morality, or moral judgment. As we will see, while Jesus has strong words of warning to the rich in countless Gospel verses, he also tends to avoid overgeneralized condemnation of them. The rich are simply the poor with more money. I do not subscribe to a moral hierarchy that imbues the poor with moral superiority, nor do I subscribe to one that places the poor at the bottom due to their economic inferiority. In other words, every effort will be taken throughout this project to avoid moralistic arguments that place a distance between rich and poor based on anything except economic reality. The rich are not inherently bad, and the poor are not intrinsically good. These are economic terms, not moral categories of good and evil. Further, to proceed through this project effectively we must also resist the temptation to idealize abject poverty as a higher moral, ethical, or spiritual good. Abject poverty is brutal, ugly, and dehumanizing. Wealth can be detrimental to the soul, but it can also be good for the body; it can be just fine for the soul, but terrible for the body. The same statements could be said of poverty. These aren't the kinds of categories that really matter much to this project, and neither are their moralizing counterparts.

I am also deeply indebted to the teachers and mentors who have fostered my passion and curiosity for this work. A pair of these are old mentors, who, despite their own marvelous capacities for complex language and five-syllable philosophical/theological jargon, taught me that if you can't explain an idea with basic language and everyday examples then you probably don't really understand the thing. As such, where possible, I will try to move forward without too much insider language, church speak, or theological jargon. At the heart of my philosophy as a preacher, for example, is the hope that my work raises the theological tradition to the dignity of human experience, rather than speaking down to the masses of everyday experience from the heights of church-insider speak. I suspect that I've come up short here already but will do my best. The point is this: if we can't begin to articulate a meaningful structure of church that makes sense to those cheesemongers and bartenders I used to work alongside, then the project fails.

Finally, it should also be noted that there are some who argue emphatically that the pastor has no place generally in the field of politics or governance, and to be a clergyperson is to stand outside of the structures of power to attend to the souls therein. In other words, the pastor should stay *above the fray*, and that a project of political applications and mechanisms is one furthest from the imaginable realm of pastoral ministry. There's not much that I can say within this space to convince the reader otherwise, except to note the ways that clergypersons, most notably Martin Luther King Jr. in recent memory, have harnessed the prophetic imagination of their sacred stories and texts toward the betterment of the communities in which they serve by way of politics. In the words of Jeffrey Stout, "The pastor has the prophetic task of declaring to the peoples of the world . . . that they are responsible for the arrangements they have made for themselves and thus for whatever injustices those arrangements entail."[9] Examining the ways, for example, that church communities and pastors helped to

---

9. Stout, *Blessed Are the Organized*, 201.

empower communities in the post-Katrina world of New Orleans, Stout finds that pastoral vision and prophetic imagination an invaluable part of this work. "The church," he writes, "must hold the people and their rulers responsible for the injustices they have perpetrated and permitted."[10] A book on civil structures that do and do not lift a particularly Christian attitude toward the poor, then, is well within range of this task. Further, following Stout, this work may very well flow out of not only the prophetic imagination of biblical scholarship, but the very center of my ordination vows as a clergyperson.

Speaking of pastoral context, it's important to note how deeply this book was inspired by the members of my present pastoral context, Shepherd of the Valley Lutheran Church in La Mesa, California. One of the ministries that arose out of the COVID-19 pandemic was a Bible study group that met on Zoom throughout lockdown. We figured that since we had nowhere else to be, we could read Matthew's Gospel at whatever pace we wanted, usually a section or two at a time over an hour or so each week. We finally finished Matthew over twenty-four months later. That group, more than almost any other, inspired this project. During our Bible study, we gathered not only across distances via Zoom, but across socioeconomic class and political background, and I couldn't help but marvel, as so many pastors do, at the faithfulness and curiosity of each person. It was a faithfulness whose resignation to the church's one-dimensional relationship with the poor through charity troubled me, as I could see it troubled many of them. They wondered if Jesus wasn't calling for something more, even if that realization made them personally uncomfortable, or might upset something of their own relationship to wealth.

In what follows, an argument through something I call *ptoxocracy* emerges, then, not as a criticism of the rich, but out of deep pastoral concern for them. As a day-to-day practitioner of theology, I am constantly improvising ways to express God's love in the world. I've seen the ways that wealth (and poverty, for that matter) can damage the soul, and ptoxocracy emerges as a healing balm, in hope that the church might find a more fulfilling expression of herself. In reclaiming her treasure, I hope the church reclaims herself.

Ptoxocracy is likely a new word to the reader, and though the pages of this book attempt a comprehensive examination of the idea, a concise definition is helpful here as the reader begins to embark on this exploration.

---

10. Stout, *Blessed Are the Organized*, 201.

INTRODUCTION

Ptoxocracy, (pronounced *p·toeks·AW·kruh·see*) is governance by the materially poor; a hybrid form of representative democracy whereby only persons of the lowest economic status are eligible for elected public office. We will return to this concise definition again in chapter 3.

Finally, and probably because I am a pastor whose Lutheran preaching professors thumped it into my head constantly, a word about our starting point.

We begin in grace. More particularly, we must begin in graciousness. We begin in the reality of God's abundant love for all creation. We *must* begin in grace extended to rich and poor alike, a delight of God so big that it washes over all people, rich and poor alike. The starting point of this work must be the tenderness of God's love that Zechariah sings, and the psalmists' limitless dwelling in God's delight. When we find that point, when it becomes so raw and clear to us that we can't do anything but bask in its joy, we are drawn to another question: so what? This is the question I hear from my parishioners all the time. It's the same question I heard from the cheesemongers and bartenders years ago in the outskirts of Chicago. *So what?*

Grace is a nonnegotiable for me, and I invite the reader to return to grace when and where they feel particularly challenged by this work. Those challenges may arise in feelings of guilt or anger, frustration, mistrust of the author as without any authority to make his arguments, and more. Yet I encourage, and I hope, that the reader will return to grace as the foundation to the possibilities in the pages to come as we wrestle with the question of where that same grace might take us. We must begin in grace, certain of God's love for the marginalized, the rich, the poor, gay, straight, cis, hetero, trans, or any other group of persons.

This book begins where other projects of theology end, in grace. It begins here in hopes of preserving an expression of God's saving grace for our children. Like Lawrence, I imagine that readers sincerely hope to embody this grace in the world and chose to pick up this book with the aim of doing just that. As we enter a vision of what might be, by way of what is and what has been, we do so in the tender reality of grace as our guide.

1

The Poor Are Always Forgotten

*For the needy shall not always be forgotten,
nor shall the hope of the poor be taken away.*

— Psalm 9:18, *Evangelical Lutheran Worship*

THE POOR ARE ALWAYS FORGOTTEN. No matter how often the psalm is quoted, prayed, or sung, the lives of the poor are treated as refuse in the ambiguous stew of human systems. Much as we desire to be good people with charitable, well-intentioned hearts toward every human being, the truth is that some lives do not matter as much as others.

It's like this.

The first time I had a conversation about a strange virus emerging in Wuhan, China, in early March 2020, I found myself laughing. A close friend was visiting us from Chicago, and we'd decided to spend a few days together (badly) attempting our hand at surfing the late-winter beaches of Southern California. A massive British Airlines Boeing 747 approached San Diego as we sat in traffic on the I-5 corridor downtown, the city's sole connection from London's Heathrow Airport. As the whistle of its engines grew louder, we listened to reports on public radio that an emerging virus would likely impact daily life for Americans, altering travel plans and shutting down industrial sectors across the world. We couldn't believe it and marveled at the audacity of reporters who were making such wild claims. We were baffled at the thought of something as trivial as a little flu-like sickness jamming a stick in the spokes of the global economy, a system we took as a given, as the jet continued over us to touch down on the runway.

My friend had been attending twelve-step meetings for just over eighteen months and was at the point of his sobriety where he could make jokes about his experience. "Coronavirus?" he said with a laugh, turning down the volume, "most of the guys I hang out with have had some form of that their whole lives! I know a guy who has had Tequila Fever pretty bad for years. I used to have the Bud Flu, in fact!" We laughed, pointing to the jet now taxiing to the terminal. It seemed to signify the unstoppable might of globalization unfurling around us.

It turns out that as he and I were joking about Bud Flu, governments and authorities were taking the virus with increasing seriousness, and that elected representatives of the US government had begun receiving confidential briefings on the matter nearly a month earlier. By the time we were driving back home after a day in the surf, those in power were well informed of the future havoc this virus might bring. Outside the halls of power, the world of punditry raged in debate as to whether the coming virus was a hoax, an existential threat, or to what degree one ought to be concerned. Masks were laughably out of the question, even to those inclined to take the virus seriously.

Hearing this report, I reluctantly emailed my small Lutheran congregation to let them know that, despite our confidence that everything would be just fine, the leaders of the church were taking the situation seriously. We would decide whether and how to cancel worship for a few weeks until the storm of virus contamination passed once we had more information. We promised to monitor the situation closely. The day my friend flew safely home to Chicago, I received a call to the hospital near my church to visit an elderly parishioner who had been experiencing shortness of breath. I donned my pastoral collar and went, worrying that this bout of pneumonia might spell trouble for the older man. Having just dropped my friend off at the airport, joking about Tequila Fever as we said goodbye, I was shocked to see hospital staff working to cordon off areas with plastic. Something monumental was happening around me. Medical staff were decked out from head to foot in personal protective gear as they taped off hallways and rooms from one another. Staff were beginning to direct patients to a single entry, apart from their families. Patients were not yet advised to wear masks, but a palpable sense of professionally contained panic was emerging around the hospital wing. I made my visit, said some prayers, was grateful that the old man was in good spirits, and left, much more shaken than when I had entered. As I walked back to my car, I noted a new structure going up hastily in the parking lot, clearly demarcating a quarantine zone of sorts.

The next day the World Health Organization declared a global pandemic, with the United States quickly following suit. We called an emergency church-council session, and I fumbled to host my first-ever Zoom meeting. Our church leaders decided to cancel worship that Sunday out of what we were still sure was an over-abundance of caution. We also decided to close the church preschool, sending just over one hundred and twenty kids home that Friday with expectations set that we'd be back open once normalcy resumed, likely in two weeks.

Yet normalcy never really returned. More than five years later, a conservative estimate from the Centers for Disease Control puts the number of US deaths attributed to complications from the COVID-19 virus at over one million people. Global numbers are harder to pinpoint, with the World Health Organization figuring no fewer than seven million. Here's where the psalmist's expression takes on its most poignant edge: most of the dead here in the United States and around the world would be the poor, marginalized, elderly, and people of color. The most vulnerable, the most easily discarded, would be treated as an afterthought. Affluent and powerful persons would be affected, and even two US presidents would contract the disease while in office. But where sitting presidents and wealthy persons had access to medical care, vaccines, and cutting-edge treatments, the poor would largely have no access to much of anything.

When the psalmist cries out, "Let not the needy be forgotten," it is an expression of exactly this sense of things, of a structural ambivalence within the halls of power that forgets the lives of the poor. In praying that the "hope of the poor" not be forgotten, the psalmist unequivocally asserts this fact, unchanged nearly three millennia later. We pray, in other words, that the hope of the poor is not taken away, that the needy not be forgotten, precisely because the reality of this world is exactly opposite: the poor are always forgotten.

THE ANATOMY OF A CHASM: LAZARUS, THE RICH MAN, AND THE COVID-19 PANDEMIC

In the Gospel of Luke, Jesus tells a parable of a man named Lazarus who, during his earthly life, lies at the gate of a rich man. The heart-wrenching circumstance of his poverty is typified when Jesus notes that "the dogs would come and lick his sores" (Luke 16:21b). In the parable, both the rich man and Lazarus die. In a drastic reversal of fortunes, the rich man now languishes in Sheol and Lazarus rests in the bosom of Abraham. When the rich man cries out for help to Lazarus from the depths of Sheol, Abraham responds to him on Lazarus's behalf: "Child, remember that during your lifetime you received your good things and Lazarus in like manner evil things, but now he is comforted here, and you are in agony. Besides all this, between you and us a *great chasm* has been fixed, so that those who might want to pass from here to you cannot do so, and no one can cross from there to us" (Luke 16:25–26; italics mine). While their fortunes have been reversed, one fact of their relationship remains the same in the logic of the parable: the *great chasm*. The nature of this chasm is what we now seek to explore—that is, the amnesia or ambivalence of the rich toward the poor in life that deepens an uncrossable terrain between us.

Lest we relegate the thrust of this parable to biblical history, the COVID-19 pandemic revealed, though it did not create, a great chasm once again, a fixed space between rich and poor through which neither can cross. The pandemic, so fresh in the minds of many of us, serves as a ready illustration of the nature of this chasm. During the early stages of the pandemic the poor could not attain adequate care, personal protective equipment, or trustworthy information about the disease. The rich, on the contrary, were generally able to access these with relative ease and speed. In the words of Jesuit priest Gregory Boyle, the COVID-19 pandemic made clear that "inequality is not a defect in the system. It is the system."[1]

Yet it wasn't just access to medical goods or services in the pandemic that came to define the chasm between rich and poor. We now know that elected representatives of the US government received confidential briefings of relative clarity about the potential dangers of COVID. One of those briefed confidentially on the matter was North Carolina senator Robert Burr, first elected in 2004. The SEC's investigations into Senator Burr later revealed that he received confidential briefings on the COVID pandemic as early as February 13, 2020, nearly an entire month before the World Health Organization declared a global pandemic.[2]

It is reasonable that elected officials should have access to information before the wider public, yet what they did with that information clarifies

---

1. Boyle, *Whole Language*, xi.
2. Kelly, "S.E.C. Inquiry."

the nature of the chasm between rich and poor. Four elected senators who had received such confidential briefings made significant trades of their stock portfolios within days and hours of these meetings. These stock trades predicted the financial devastation that the virus would wreak on certain sectors in their portfolios, especially travel and hotel stocks, with the kind of mystifying clarity that reeked of insider trading.[3] Later, when under investigation for these actions, one senator was so audacious in his defense that he did not even deny the explicit connection between the sale of his vast holdings in hotel and travel stocks to the confidential reports he had heard in the halls of power.[4] While my friend and I joked about the Bud Flu and Tequila Fever, adrift in a stew of misinformation and confusion, elected leaders were busy employing their confidential knowledge with an aim at advancing their own personal interests.

Consider these actions another way: during the nineteen years Robert Burr served as a senator from North Carolina, the United States invested billions in intricate technological systems whose primary function is to warn coastal cities of impending tsunamis. In the face of a potential tsunami, seconds and minutes can mean the difference between life or death, and within seconds of the mere possibility of impending danger, alarms begin to ring for coastal communities. One cannot help but wonder how the course of the global pandemic might have played out in the United States if its elected leaders—that is, those with direct access to power by way of financial resources, legislative authority, federal emergency powers, and other sophisticated resources of the wealthiest nation in the world—had spent the twenty-plus days between receiving confidential intelligence and the declaration of a global pandemic actually ringing alarm bells.

Yet in the days between the briefings of US senators and the declaration of the pandemic, no unified alarms were sounded in poor communities. Instead, the rich traded on their inside information, and the poor were forgotten, left without care, access, or even helpful information. Worse, the poor were left to wade through a myriad of disinformation, much of it coming from the same high places, from the very members of Congress and the federal branches who had received classified details of the impending virus. Early advocacy and education of communities, whether teaching about proper mask usage in February 2020 (having learned that the disease was airborne and largely preventable with good ventilation and masking during

3. Slodysko, "Sen. Burr Under Investigation."
4. Kelly, "S.E.C. Inquiry."

those confidential meetings), might have yielded a lower death toll among this highly vulnerable population. Yet instead of educating the public about proper ventilation in the event of a deadly airborne illness, stockpiling resources, and bringing community leaders together, these same leaders spent their energy publicly arguing about the efficacy of masks, even as first waves of the virus crashed on the wider public, spurring the kinds of ambiguities that conspiracy theorists would use to great advantage in sowing further political discord.

What's worse is that these same officials seem also to have proven immune from consequences for their actions. The Department of Justice eventually dropped charges of insider trading. One legal expert cited the numerous frameworks of constitutional clauses that are "meant to shield federal lawmakers from criminal prosecutions or civil actions related to their legislative work" as a probable factor in the DOJ's closure of the case.[5] While senatorial actions may have been morally reprehensible, a complex network of laws protected them from the consequences of their actions as members of the ruling class. Elected officials were held to no account for the failings of their moral instincts, swept aside so easily by the urgent concerns of their personal financial interests.

It would have been enough if COVID had been a historical outlier, still meriting serious consideration of structural deficiencies in our governing bodies. Jeffrey Stout's 2010 work, *Blessed Are the Organized*, examines a similar set of disturbing ways in which the rich profited from Hurricane Katrina's 2005 devastation of New Orleans at the expense of the poor in the storm's aftermath. This pattern is neither novel nor is it new; thus again does the psalmist cry for the poor's mere remembrance, as if the defining characteristic of this great chasm is the amnesia that it produces in the rich. The global pandemic of COVID-19 and the devastation of Hurricane Katrina are not the first times that the rich have forgotten the poor, nor are they the first times that enrichment of a wealthy ruling class would be had at the expense of the poor. This is the nature of the great chasm in Jesus's parable, the intentional and systemic divide between those whose lives matter and those whose lives do not.

I will take this statement one step further and say that what this retrospective reveals as the defining characteristic of the system, the nature of this chasm between rich and poor, is a characteristic that finally became

---

5. Kelly, "S.E.C. Inquiry," para. 14.

desperately clear during the early days of the pandemic: the rich have little or no meaningful stake in the lives of the poor.

When I say that the rich have no stake in the lives of the poor, I have in mind something akin to holding an interest, as a businessperson might hold a share of stock in a company. This framing of the issue is one to which we will return throughout this book. By *stake* I mean the sort of thing that wealthy elected officials attended to after their confidential briefings. As a stakeholder, one seeks to increase the value of a stock by any legal means necessary. These means include both everyday ethical and legal actions, as well as morally dubious (though legal) practices like short selling, or, as it turns out, insider trading by governing representatives on confidential information. Whatever the means, one does not hold stock in a company simply for the fun of holding the stock; rather, one holds stock with the aim of increasing the value of one's overall portfolio. Holding stock means possessing a tangible interest in the well-being, profitability, or high functioning of the enterprise. Like other rich persons, I hold a stake in the outcome of multiple companies and governments by way of a mixture of retirement investment accounts.

The pandemic helps to see clearly what is usually obscured in day-to-day life, that when faced with a true existential threat, rich leaders did what was most logical as stakeholders: they looked to the well-being of their interests. They had no reason not to act this way, and even less of a reason to attend to the needs of the poor, because they had no stake in the lives of the poor beyond a vague and often contradictory set of moral imperatives. While this might strike some as morally reprehensible, it is perfectly legal: the elected officials ignoring the poor are acting as one might reasonably expect a person with resources to protect might act—that is, in protection and advancement of their own personal holdings.

Lest we be too hard on those who seek the well-being of their interests in the time of crisis, it is only fair to remember that most of us (me included) worried about our retirement accounts in those early days of the pandemic, watching the value of those interests plummet as international markets tanked. But most of us differ from those briefed members of Congress in a significant way: the elected representatives had access to the kinds of information that could have saved lives weeks earlier. Excusing them for inaction is like excusing a geologist who raises no alarm after their measurements warn of an impending tsunami. It is a problem of accountability.

Yet representative democracy can make no account for the interests of the poor, and members of Congress were not held responsible for their failures. In other words, the system worked exactly as it was designed to work. The fact of the matter is, however, that nothing about our governmental structure gave our leaders a meaningful stake in the lives of poor. Holding these leaders accountable for their actions might accomplish this task, yet all these representatives were relieved of accountability by the Justice Department, signaling to future rich elected officials that their actions were perfectly normative within the system's design. The chasm is defined by the givenness of these actions, that there is little accountability for those who forget the poor.

THE FEEBLENESS OF MORAL IMPERATIVES

Stepping back from national political drama, perhaps another example will help get to what is meant in framing the problem as the rich have no meaningful stake in the lives of the poor. These kinds of situations happen all the time, and acknowledging the ways that our personal or organizational interests drive our individual actions can help lend a sense of perspective.

For this example, it is helpful to know that as the pastor, I am one voting member of ten on the board of my church. This means that constitutionally speaking, I play a role on the board as one of ten fiduciaries. This fiduciary duty is quite a different thing than a moral imperative based on my theological convictions, ordination vows, and personal beliefs. In fact, as practically every pastor I know will confess, there are times when the fiduciary duty comes into explicit conflict with these moral imperatives.

The tension is felt acutely in my dealings with unhoused persons when they arrive at the church seeking food, shelter, or money. My congregation runs a large preschool and after-school program serving over one hundred families in our communities, a program that is central to our mission. This is both a ministry we undertake for the sake of the community and a financial necessity for the congregation, making it a win-win situation for both local parents seeking great childcare and our church budget. To run a successful preschool, however, we need to operate in accordance with all California State childcare licensing requirements that, for good reason, strongly prioritize the safety of children above nearly every other concern. These licensing requirements make certain activities that may directly pose a risk to children on the same premises difficult, though not impossible.

The presence of unhoused persons on our property, say by way of a food bank or resource center, presents exactly the kind of risk that licensing thoroughly discourages. In other words, these licensing requirements heighten our stake in the safe-keeping of children, which is ultimately a very good thing.

Now, as nearly every pastor can attest, there are days when hungry persons come knocking at the door, no matter what we've done to dissuade them from doing so. Ordinarily church staff would have some funds or processes through which they could provide individuals with food, give cash or goods, and so on. Yet because of my fiduciary duty to the organization, one that understands this hungry person to be endangering the childcare licensing requirements that financially and missionally underpin our interests, this means that I am presented with a moral conundrum: do I feed the hungry person per my moral imperative, and put my church in jeopardy of losing our childcare license, or do I send him away empty handed so that I can preserve the fiduciary responsibility to the mission and financial interests of the organization?

My point here is not to highlight the moral dilemmas of pastors. Pastors are not unlike most people in this respect. We all face moral dilemmas and will continue to be more than capable of navigating life's questions in ways that satisfy both the letter and spirit of the law. (In this case it is easy to lovingly escort the hungry person off my grounds, fill up his gas tank at the local gas station, buy him groceries, and send him on his way out of town, all while keeping kids safe on the church property). However, my point is this: the rich have nothing akin to a fiduciary duty toward or within the lives of the poor in the same way that I have a fiduciary duty as a member of a board of my church. This means that, more often than not, the demands of one's moral imperatives become secondary to their fiduciary counterparts. Because my congregation counts on those preschool dollars to stay financially solvent, I am admittedly likelier to prioritize my fiduciary duty than feed the hungry person in front of me. There is little beyond cultural or traditional norms holding leaders like me to a higher standard of behavior toward the poor, and in some cases, there is a bias for their behavior toward the poor that may, in fact, dissuade us from helping.

Another example will help illustrate what I mean here and given the touchy nature of this subject, it's best that I select another example from my personal experience. A few years ago, my wife and I purchased our first home in the eastern suburbs of San Diego. Southern California real estate was difficult to break into, and we were outbid or rejected in our offers to buy homes in the area several times. Like most millennial first-time homeowners, we had to borrow from family to satisfy terms and conditions with our loan officer to become eligible for a loan.

When the loan came through and the purchase agreement for our first home was finalized, we became financial partners with the bank in holding a vested interest in the value and well-being of the property. This interest has formed my actions in the years since we made the purchase. I not only make monthly mortgage payments, but I've installed solar panels and re-landscaped the home to make it less prone to wildfires and drought, both as a result of moral commitments to environmental good and as economic decisions. As an investor and interest-holder in my property, I have decided that it is not only economically good for me to care for my property and make monthly payments, but I hope that eventually the value of my home will be more, not less, than the amount I pay to the bank for the original loan upon selling it. I have an economic interest, in other words, in acting in accord with these duties. I suspect that there's nothing unusual here, and that my behavior is relatively normative.

Holding a meaningful interest gives rise to new perspectives. Earthquakes are more consequential to me now as a homeowner in Southern California than they ever were as a renter, for example, because most home insurance policies don't cover earthquake damages. So, after we bought the home, I started thinking about earthquakes more seriously because we live in an earthquake-prone area. My interest in my home has altered the ways I navigate threats, advantages, and everything in between, and I acknowledge that it has changed the way I think about neighborhoods, school districts, fire stations, and other civic structures.

Yet it wasn't just earthquakes that started to keep me up at night as a stakeholder in this sizable investment. Prior to my investment I considered myself an advocate for the unhoused and found myself appalled at the ways in which home-owning families spoke about unhoused persons outside their doors. Sadly, my instincts as a homeowner—that is, a shareholder whose vested interest seeks a positive financial outcome for my holdings—have changed my behavior toward the unhoused. Outside my home there are frequently unhoused persons on the street, and panhandling individuals walking around the highway entrance down the road. These numbers appear to have increased since we made our purchase. We've even had some of these persons fall asleep or call out to us in a medical emergency on the edges of our property. Now, since home valuation is derived, in part, from sale values of other approximate homes in the area, the mere presence of these unhoused persons is not just a moral problem, it becomes a financial problem. Unhoused persons are a drag on home value because they potentially dissuade future buyers exploring the neighborhood from entering the market, thus driving down home values. The mere existence of these persons in my neighborhood therefore opposes my financial interests. Again, I am assuming that my financial interests here are normative, and that no one wishes their investments to decrease in value.

The poor therefore become an enemy to homeowners because of their potential for negative consequences on one's interests. The problem is addressed in local governments by means of disincentivizing the physical signs of poverty in the area. Municipalities do this by making panhandling illegal, establishing gates for communities, placing uncomfortable railings on park benches, or they enact measures that empower law enforcement to harass these individuals. In other words, as a homeowner, I hold the opposite of having a stake in the lives of the poor, as does my local government who takes these actions. Because we are stakeholders in our property values and by extension our family's long-term success by way of the continued increase of that property value, we become stakeholders whose obligations to our holdings place our interests opposite the interests of the poor themselves.

Let's take it a step further. The wealthier the person, the less a meaningful stake in the lives of the poor one holds, because the complicated web of financial commitments and fiduciary duties grows with an increased number of interests. The more shares of properties, businesses, and interests one has, the less likely one can truly have a stake in the lives of the poor because of a growing number of fiduciary responsibilities. This extends not only to homeownership but into business; the poor are as bad for business as they are for home valuations for these same reasons.

Both of these examples demonstrate the way that moral imperatives fail to impart a meaningful stake in the lives of the poor in this way: I may hold certain convictions as a person of faith, as an ordained leader in the church, or as a generally kindhearted person, but all of these become secondary to the normative experience as a fiduciary. In the face of fiduciary duties, moral imperatives fail to impart a meaningful stake in the lives of the poor because while moral imperatives are optional, fiduciary duties entail structures of accountability. I am accountable to both my board (in the first example) and to my bank (in the second example) in ways that I am not structurally accountable to poor persons in either example. A moral imperative to do good lacks a means to supply a meaningful interest in the lives of the poor that would supersede the fiduciary duty to which I will be held publicly accountable.

CHARITY AND MORAL IMPERATIVES: THE MOS MAIORUM OF OUR TIMES

It was not until late in its existence that the Roman Republic codified laws into written form, as we might expect a republic to function successfully today by way of constitutions and written laws. What held the Republic together until the early first century BC were a set of "unwritten rules, traditions, and mutual expectations collectively known as *mos maiorum*."[6] Literally translated into "the way of the elders," the *mos maiorum* dictated expectations for persons of every station in society. These rules encompassed everything in government from the ways that bills and measures might arrive for discussion in the Senate to the unquestionably problematic presence of armed troops within the inner sanctums of Rome itself at the invitation of one of its politicians. "Even as political rivals competed for wealth and power, their shared respect for the strength of the client-patron relationship, the sovereignty of the Assemblies, and the wisdom of the Senate kept them from going too far."[7] Surprisingly, the *mos maiorum* functioned effectively for an exceptionally long run of Roman Republican history, serving to balance the various interests of ruling powers in times of conflict.

Until they didn't. The moment political actors realized the expediency in flaunting *mos maiorum*, the Republic entered into times of deep crisis. Historian Mike Duncan notes the civil war that broke out in the late Roman Republic centered on exactly this problem. "When the Republic began to break down in the late second century it was not the letter of Roman law that eroded, but the respect for the mutually accepted bonds of *mos maiorum*."[8] Faced with civil and military crises on multiple fronts, accepted norms of right and wrong in civil discourse were not strong enough forces to counter developing threats to the Roman Republic. Time and again, the Republic

6. Duncan, *Storm Before the Storm*, 4.
7. Duncan, *Storm Before the Storm*, 4.
8. Duncan, *Storm Before the Storm*, 4.

was forced to witness the open flaunting of the norms of *mos maiorum* at the hands of the Gracchi brothers, Sulla, and Marius, as the Republic slid toward open despotism. Even after the crises subsided, future leaders like Pompey the Great, Crassus, and Julius Caesar learned a terrible lesson that would resonate across Roman history from that moment onward. Social norms like the *mos maiorum*, unlike written rules, could be tossed aside at the whims of political expediency. These would also be the same persons who drove the final nails in the coffin for the Republic, ascendants who understood the weakness of normative expectations in power politics.

Charity and moral imperatives function as the *mos maiorum* of our time. One cannot be forced to behave altruistically toward the poor, or to possess a meaningful stake in the lives of the poor. As such, political actors are held to no account in forgetting the poor at the service of political expediency.

This is what I take to be one of the central premises of Reinhold Niebuhr's *Moral Man and Immoral Society*, in which Niebuhr reflected that power "is a poison which blinds the eyes of moral insight and lames the will of moral purpose."[9] Morality is a toothless custom that constantly yields to the responsibilities of self-interest. Such collective goodness of attitude toward the poor would require mass education and action, nearly totalitarian in scope, which Niebuhr rightly rejects as plausible. "All men," he writes, "cannot be expected to become spiritual any more than they can be expected to become rational."[10] Any representative system that is expected to function best when all its voting population are educated, moral, and altruistic is one that will ultimately fail in addressing a broad array of interests beyond those of the most powerful. Mass education for civic good are the tools of totalitarian regimes, not democracies.

One might argue that representative democracy provides the opportunity to do better morally in relation to the poor—that is, to elect persons of ethically high value systems. One might argue that democratic elections give the opportunity to elect persons whose moral commitments see practices like insider trading and short-selling as reprehensible, and that such opportunities function as forms of accountability in representative democracy. This is certainly a possibility, and one that has indeed born historical counterexamples. American civil rights activist and politician John Lewis, the Georgia Fifth District's representative to the US House of

9. Niebuhr, *Moral Man and Immoral Society*, 6.
10. Niebuhr, *Moral Man and Immoral Society*, 73.

Representatives from 1987 until his death in 2020, seems a perfect example of the kind of ruling leader that democratic society can produce when functioning at its moral finest. Yet it takes an awful lot of representatives like John Lewis to undo the damage that can be created by others within a representational government, and it is hard to make a case that Congress has ever known a majority of representatives with the moral spine of Lewis.

Further, as Thomas Vazzo writes, "The poor are not really a voting bloc or a contributing one,"[11] and electing enough leaders with moral courage is a challenge that democracy has yet to overcome in practice. As such, the interests of the poor fall relatively low in the hierarchy of society's interests, because the one mechanism that could hold the rich accountable (that is, reelection), is beyond their significant participation.

We might also counter that moral training can produce persons with high ethical standards who might be elected in the future, that the mere possibility of Lewis's election to the House gives a glimmer of hope. Such arguments are pervasive among folks like me, whose livelihoods depend on training future leaders through theological, ethical, and moral frameworks. For many years this was exactly the logic many faithful churchgoers had in attending church, and which pastors took to be their purpose. Churchgoers might not have agreed with everything their pastor was saying in the pulpit, and—*gasp!*—they may not even hold to many of the wider denomination's theological commitments when pushed, yet there was a sense that many people continue to go to one church or another simply to learn how to be a better person in the world. As one churchgoer put it to me, "I think that church could just be summed up in a few words: don't be a jerk." Such an argument presumes that the value of institutions like church or higher education function as mechanisms toward these ends, as moral training grounds meant to instill values that mirror the social capacity of Rome's *mos maiorum* in much of its Republican history.

There are numerous problems with these assumptions, though two primary problems arise. Let's suppose that the church, it's values, and other ethical commitments continue their present trajectory, and that charity and ethical training continue to be one (of many) byproducts of denominational Christianity in the United States, a kind of *mos maiorum* for a broad—even if disparate—body of citizens. Could this be enough of a guardrail against a lack of stakeholders in the life of the poor? Unfortunately, I believe the answer is no, and that it proves to be an overreliance on the good will that

---

11. Vozzo, *Homeboy Way*, 159.

such training can generate in the best of times when these institutions are functioning highly. For one, these institutions have never, nor will they ever, provide a unified understanding of charity and moral imperative. My denomination outrightly rejects the idea of moral training as its primary purpose on the grounds of theological commitments, for example.

The assumption further ignores the fact that it is precisely these institutions that are in significant historical decline presently, and in their place movements of Christian extremism are growing, especially in their political power. These growing movements explicitly pronounce antidemocratic, pro-theocratic aims, and are on the rise.[12] "At this point," writes *The Atlantic's* Stephanie McCrummen, "tens of millions of believers—about 40 percent of American Christians, including Catholics, according to a recent Denison University survey—are embracing an alluring, charismatic movement that has little use for religious pluralism, individual rights, or constitutional democracy." If we expect a declining set of apolitical and ununified institutions to reinforce a set of uncodified moral attitudes like charity toward the poor, institutions which are fading in moral influence as it is, then we face a similar crisis of dismay to that of the late-Republic Romans. Unwritten codes of morality do not constitute interests that can sustain the barrage of self-interests.

Charity and moral training constitute norms rather than a structures. When push comes to shove, it is structure and law, as well as the appetites of ascendent political figures, which will always supersede the relatively weak power of norms. This is why, for example, Ibram X. Kendi argues that antiracist policy changes must precede the work of "changing of hearts and minds" against racist attitudes. It is why he writes that "the original problem of racism has not been solved by suasion. Knowledge is only power if knowledge is put to the struggle for power. Changing minds is not a movement . . . if a person has no record of power or policy change, then that person is not an activist."[13] So long as we rely on cultural norms to impart interests in the lives of the poor, we will continue to actively engage in wishful thinking over tangible outcome.

Charity is an optional norm and not an actual interest, and continues to fail in addressing the reality and depths of actual poverty because it lacks the capacity to hold the wealthy accountable to their claims of concern to the poor, much as unwritten political norms eventually fail to hold despots

---

12. McCrummen, "Army of God Comes Out," para. 8.
13. Kendi, *How to Be an Anti-Racist*, 209.

accountable. It was until quite recently the custom of those hoping to ascend to the highest office in the United States to release a certain number of tax filings so that the voting public might more transparently understand the source of their wealth. More important than what those filings showed, according to the logic of the custom, was the act of good faith itself. In demonstrating subservience to a time-honored tradition of transparency, another flailing *mos maiorum* of our time, voters could decide whether the potential candidate was qualified for the office by way of an ambiguous claim to morality. Charity fails the poor in the way that the *mos maiorum* failed the late-Republic Romans. It would be of no surprise to men like Sulla and the Gracchi brothers that a recent presidential nominee blatantly flaunted the democratic customs of running for office. Charity falls short because it is a custom precisely in the way that releasing one's tax records is a custom, precisely in the way that Sulla eventually defied the *mos maiorum* of Roman life by bringing a legion of soldiers into the inner sanctum of the city. Eventually the political actor who does not want to take part in the custom simply refuses to do so.

CHARITY: AN APPEARANCE OF CARE THAT STYMIES ACTUAL CARE

We must nuance this discussion of meaningful interests in the lives of the poor with one final point—namely, that there is one way in which charity does serve as an interest in the lives of the rich. In the words of Reinhold Niebuhr, charity functions for the rich man as "at once a display of his power and an expression of his pity,"[14] which is to say that the public act of charity is the means of demonstrating one's personal wealth to other persons. This is another problem with charity: the poor are only remembered when the rich are directly affected; that is, when the rich seek to appear generous, they often turn to the poor as a means of boosting their worth by way of public prestige or tax benefits. In this way the rich turn the poor into a means of their continued self-enrichment rather than valuing the poor as ends in themselves. Niebuhr goes on to address the ways the rich express their befuddlement at the poor when the latter respond to the failings of charity: "If the disinherited treat these gestures with cynicism and interpret unconscious sentimentality as conscious hypocrisy, the privileged will be properly outraged and offended by the moral perversity of the recipients

---

14. Niebuhr, *Moral Man and Immoral Society*, 14.

of their beneficences."[15] A true interest in the poor recognizes the systemic nature of poverty as well as the relative impotence of charity in the face of this structural deficiency.

Oftentimes the public is told that the complexities of poverty make it an unchangeable situation. Citing Jesus, we will be piously reminded that "the poor you will always have with you," and that no structural changes would be enormous enough to counter the historical weight of poverty. These arguments are as feeble as charity itself. Make no mistake that policymakers could decide to tackle poverty in the way that, say, they prioritized the American financial system during its 2007 meltdown. Matthew Desmond's 2023 book, *Poverty, by America*, for example, offers a well-thought-out articulation of just such a set of policy measures that, were they taken in turn, could seriously alter the landscape of American income inequality. Desmond offers one concrete solution after another in this text, solutions that are not only sound in theory but whose empirical foundations have been proven historically. The solutions to the alleviation of poverty are there, yet, as Desmond points out repeatedly, most of these policy measures have a single enemy: the rich elected officials who have no stake in the outcomes or effectiveness of such policies. There are a myriad number of great policy measures we could enact that would alleviate the hardships of poverty, but the hurdle in doing so is the interests of the wealthy. When he writes, "The American government gives the most help to those who need it least,"[16] Desmond is not being hyperbolic: a steady-handed empirical foundation of research guides his work. Considering forms of taxes in sum, Desmond concludes that "the four hundred richest Americans are taxed at 23 percent, the lowest rate of all."[17] Little can or will change in representative government so long as the interests of the rich are prioritized as the interests of the whole.

What would it take for the rich as rulers to hold a meaningful stake in the lives of the poor? There are plenty of possibilities, yet the political reality of enacting such measures is limited given the seamless translation of wealth into political currency, a dizzyingly unjust feedback loop that leaves the interests of the wealthy as unchallenged benefactors of political and policy priority. Yet we can envision and imagine a world in which the interests of the poor are heightened. A policy that tied capital gains tax

---

15. Niebuhr, *Moral Man and Immoral Society*, 80.
16. Desmond, *Poverty, by America*, 95.
17. Desmond, *Poverty, by America*, 95.

rates to high school dropout rates in each municipality or even nationally would likely raise the stakes for the poor. Or perhaps a national tax penalty established on those earning above the poverty rate fixed at the incarceration differentials between convicts of given ethnicities in proportion to their national population. Or we could begin by simply taking Desmond's suggestion to end the mortgage interest tax deduction (which again, disproportionately benefits the rich over the poor) and then directing the gains of that deduction toward the alleviation of poverty. These possibilities would snap the rich to attention by creating meaningful stakes in the lives of the poor in ways that charity can never, nor will it ever, create. There is a very important reason that such policies are nonexistent: the ruling class has a stake in the outcome of the rich because the ruling class is mostly made up of the rich. The ruling class has no stake, no fiduciary interest, in the lives of the poor. Until this changes, the poor will remain forgotten.

Imagine what this most powerful nation in the world might accomplish if its rich ruling class held a stake in the lives of the poor! I contend that if the rich had a meaningful stake in the lives of the poor, the United States immigration system wouldn't be such a mess. If the rich had a stake in the lives of the poor, medicine would be inexpensive and widely available equitably. If the rich had a meaningful stake in the lives of the poor, we could easily enact policies protecting communities from loan sharks, police abuse, ecological devastation, climate change, and opioid addiction. As it stands, the rich have no real reason beyond feeble moral imperative to care about the statistical fact that poor children are much more likely to die by firearms in public school, or to feel implicated in the suffering of fellow human beings who have less material worth than themselves. There is no reason that a wealthy, white, suburban American should concern themselves about low homeownership rates of Black and Brown Americans except a flaccid moral imperative encountered occasionally on social media or from a pulpit once a week. It makes no physical difference whether Black teens are more likely to be arrested on drug charges than white teens, though rates of use are identical. Jesus's great chasm exists because white suburban Americans have no stake in the well-being of poorer Black communities. Every investment is a risk, and because they hold no interests in the lives of the poor, the rich risk nothing in forgetting the poor.

Charity lacks the adequate capacity to care for the poor because it lacks true accountability. "Power," writes Jeffrey Stout, "is the capacity that an individual, group, or institution has to produce effects that people have reason to care about."[18] Charity fails to bridge the chasm between Lazarus and the rich man because it is ambiguous at best, and without any substantial mechanism of accountability. Worse, as Stout writes, "Power minus accountability equals domination."[19] Not only are the poor forgotten, but they are dominated by the rich precisely for lack of structural accountability. As a pastor, I can get as exasperated as I want when the wealthiest member of my congregation gives the smallest amount, yet beyond my moral exasperation, I am powerless in forcing their hand to give more. This is probably a good thing in the case of pastors and their parishioners, but in the case of civil society it means the poor exist without structures that might imbue their fellow citizens with any interest in their well-being via a mechanism of accountability.

THE PTOXOI

It is time to introduce a key term that will define our work from this point on, one which the reader has encountered already in the opening pages of this book, as well as in the root of its title: the *ptoxoi*. In biblical Greek the *ptoxoi* are the destitute, abject, and nameless poor. They are the beggars. To speak of the *ptoxoi* is to embody the world's attitude toward them, for to pronounce this word aloud in a manner true to each of its consonants, one is forced to embody a conventional attitude for these whom it defines. To speak the word *ptoxoi* aloud one must practically spit. While it is possible, at least in English, to ignore the *p* and *t* as distinct (as most English speakers pronounce the mathematician Ptolemy, for example), the most precise pronunciation of this word includes a trace of both. Two harsh consonants, one after another, make it nearly impossible to get the word out in a clean sweep without a trace of spittle on one's lips. Even if one surpasses these consonants successfully, one is forced to articulate the *x*, which performs what speech therapists call *back sounds* in the back of the throat. The back sound forced by the *x* also resembles the action of clearing one's throat. The definition of the word *ptoxoi* is performed in its utterance, first by the lips and then in the throat. The *ptoxoi* know the disdain embodied in this performance altogether too well.

In the Septuagint this word *ptoxoi* occurs in some form over one hundred times and often takes the place of a Hebrew word whose basic

18. Stout, *Blessed Are the Organized*, 55.
19. Stout, *Blessed Are the Organized*, 63.

definition is, "without an inheritance of one's own."[20] There are two words that can be translated as *the poor* in biblical Greek (or *koine* Greek, as it's called). One of these refers to the poor who are lacking in excess goods, but who can generally cover the costs of basic goods for daily life. These are the *penes*, an ahistorical match for what we would consider middle class today. However, it is fascinating to note that Jesus never employs the word *penes* in his ministry, only *ptoxoi*. In fact, Jesus tends to label all those who are not living in abject poverty as simply being *rich*, that is, the *plusioi*. The poor are contrasted, not by those with an excess of wealth and goods, but with those aristocrats who are indeed materially wealthy *and* with those whom we might even label today as middle class. *Ptoxoi* "denotes the complete destitution which forces the poor to seek the help of others by begging."[21] In other words, *penes* points toward those persons who can provide for themselves, whereas *ptoxoi* points to those abandoned by society, a category of persons that Jesus pays particular attention to.

Some scholars argue that in Jesus's time the divide between poor and rich was so drastic that there was little use for terms like *penes* anyway. One prominent scholar, Steven Friesen, suggests that the "overwhelming majority of the population under Roman imperialism lived near the subsistence level,"[22] explaining Jesus's preoccupation with their well-being. Breaking the Greco-Roman world into economic categories based on the caloric intake of each group, Friesen writes that "'[s]ubsistence level' is here defined as the resources needed to procure enough calories in food to maintain the human body."[23] He suggests that a full 28 percent, but as many as another 40 percent (for a total of around 68 percent) of those living in the era in which the New Testament was compiled lived at or below a level that would define them as the *ptoxoi*.

While any reference to the poor as qualified by an immaterial idea are well-intentioned and even have biblical and functional basis (i.e., the poor in spirit, the poor in love, the poor in heart), they are not included in our definition of the poor for this project. This kind of poverty is ambiguous, subject to manipulation, and hard to quantify. Moreover, it is a sneaky line whereby those materially wealthy can call themselves poor even when not materially poor. In the words of Gustavo Gutiérrez, speaking against an

---

20. Kittel and Friedrich, *Theological Dictionary*, s.v. "Ptoxoi."
21. Kittel and Friedrich, *Theological Dictionary*, s.v. "Ptoxoi."
22. Friesen, "Poverty in Pauline Studies," 348.
23. Friesen, "Poverty in Pauline Studies," 348.

understanding of spiritual poverty, to allow spiritual poverty in conversations of rich and poor is "to play with words—and with persons."[24] The rich can call themselves poor in spirit, and we do not intend to count them among the defined poor for this argument. The rich lay claim to enough; they need not inhabit our definitions of poverty as well.

Gutiérrez notes that whereas biblical Greek shies away from distinguishing between types of poverty beyond the *ptoxoi* and the *penes*, Hebrew is rich in vivid imagery, demonstrating how poverty is "a central theme in both the Old and the New Testaments."[25] He expresses the biblical imagination and usage of the Hebrew Bible's concern for the poor, writing,

> In the Old Testament the term which is used least to speak of the poor is *rash*, which has a rather neutral meaning. . . . [T]he prophets preferred terms which are "photographic" of real, living persons. The poor person is, therefore, *ébyôn*, the one who desires, the beggar, the one who is lacking something and who awaits it from another. He is also *dal*, the weak one, the frail one; the expression of *the poor of the land* (the rural proletariat) is found very frequently. The poor person is also *ani*, the bent over one, the one laboring under a weight, the one not in possession of his whole strength and vigor, the humiliated one. And finally he is *anew*, from the same root as the previous term but having a more religious connotation—"humble before God."[26]

This brief linguistic study demonstrates the centrality of the poor to the cultural context of the biblical imagination. The poor are at the heart of the Hebrew prophetic imagination. Just as some cultures have an excess of certain verbiage that highlights a particularly important relationship with a set of words, (as the popular, if not entirely correct assertion that Eskimos have over fifty words that can describe attributes of *snow*), an abundance of descriptive language for the poor exists in Hebrew. The poor are the frail, the weak, the bent over, the humble, the humiliated, and the begging; all these definitions from out of the prophetic tradition can help us frame and inform a conception of the *ptoxoi* as we move forward and serve to elevate concerns for the poor beyond a limited scope of thinking. A richer, more vivid set of linguistics can illuminate a more imaginative path forward.

---

24. Gutiérrez, *Theology of Liberation*, 164.
25. Gutiérrez, *Theology of Liberation*, 165.
26. Gutiérrez, *Theology of Liberation*, 165.

Which brings us to the rich. When I shorthand the rich hereafter (and have done so prior to this moment), it is meant merely to signal those of a class who have ready access to all the things that the class of the poor do not, including but not limited to stocks, money, inheritance, land, private property, business ownership, intellectual property rights, and livestock. Friesen's categories for those included within the *plusioi* extends from the small number of imperial elite to a more broad category of persons who could reasonably hope for stable caloric intake. In this regard, though I don't usually understand myself as a rich person, Friesen's categories based on caloric intake help clarify Jesus's tendency toward dualistic rich/poor categories. I easily fall within the class of *plusioi* as a white, male, middle-class landowner in Southern California with two expensive higher-education degrees from private institutions, married to a woman with full-time employment and with whom I raise two male-identifying biological children, who can reasonably expect some form of inheritance from parents and/or in-laws. Most of the persons with whom I strongly associate have similar stations in life.

When I employ the term *rich* in this project, I mean it in precisely this sense: included under the umbrella of *rich* is anyone who does not live in abject poverty, those who can reasonably expect a full caloric intake, including the *penes*. In other words, I choose to use these words dualistically, much like Jesus uses them in the Gospels. Again, my family and I fall under this category, as do most of the people with whom I associate within my church and community. Because wealth, as well as the perception of one's wealth, can be sticky issues, it's helpful to remember that the aim here is not to classify rich persons as morally dubious, and poor persons as morally superior, nor is it to idolize the condition of the poor. Quite the contrary, and the reader is encouraged to seriously examine their own position within these frames. Again, the argument that follows rests entirely outside moral assessments of rich and poor as such; relieving ourselves of moral assessments helps us to think critically about oppressive and undignified systems within which we live. The idea here is less to lay blame or a sense of righteous anger on the page, than to give voice to a group of people who generally do not have a voice, that is, the *ptoxoi*.

CONCLUSION

The *ptoxoi*, as the psalmist cries, are always forgotten. This is either by design (as Niebuhr and Boyle might argue), or at the very least an egregious yet unintentional byproduct of structural design. The structures of society function at their most efficient when they hide the poor; the system works most effectively when we actively forget them. It is designed to do this. A last thought of policy matters, though a first thought of the ruling class when they must appear humane through public acts of charity, this is a problem of generations so deep that more than three millennia ago the psalmist cries out for divine aid in helping leaders simply remember the poor. It's a low threshold to meet, but the psalmist cuts straight to the point of the problem: wealthy interests have no use for the poor except, perhaps, exploitation or cheap labor, which is a cynical interest indeed. More than that, the rich have little reason to see the poor as anything but an enemy to personal interests.

If the rich have no stake in the lives of the poor, and this is the source of our constant amnesia toward them, the question becomes what it might take for the wealthy to hold such a meaningful interest. This is the vision of ptoxocracy, arising from within the Christian tradition but whose legacy extends well beyond it. Ptoxocracy imagines a structure in which the rich are given a meaningful interest in the well-being of the lives of the poor. The immediate crisis of the 2020 pandemic may have subsided, but the true crisis of the great chasm between rich and poor that it laid bare once again has not, nor will it anytime soon be closed. Poverty isn't a defect; it is the system functioning exactly as it was designed to function. Despite our efforts to tweak and adjust the system, to aid it with moral imperatives or charity, the fact of poverty remains.

All at once the question leads to a premise that is both deeply simple, and deeply radical. The poor have been failed, even by the American experiment, so that a fundamental revision to that experiment from out of the depths of scriptural witness is necessary. By virtue of their incapacity to solve the radical inequality of American civil society, the rich have proven themselves incapable of governance, even those who claim the moral imperatives of charity as supreme. They have no stake in the lives of the poor, and no systematic means by which they could attain one. The center of American politics is wealth, and the interests of the wealthy have been and will continue to be the essential focal point for the American experiment until they are decentered. In other words, the norms of the patterns of behavior we see within American politics will continue until we actively choose to fashion a system in which those who desire personal wealth above the good of society are unable to attain political power in the first place.

2

The Mythology of the Rich Ruling Class

THE FIRST SEASON OF the Netflix hit *The Crown* revolves around Queen Elizabeth II and her ascent to power. As the season unfolds, we witness the budding monarch's reluctance to ascend the throne following the death of her father, King George VI, and we are treated to a dramatized version of events in which all characters must point to and play a part in the coronation service of the young monarch. Contemporary audiences are likely surprised at the ways church officials scoff at the scandalous possibility when the queen's husband, the Duke of Edinburgh, proposes that her coronation be televised. So sacrosanct is the coronation, they say, that it cannot be denigrated by the vulgarity of television. Yet a deal is struck after much hand wringing: the coronation may be televised, but the actual moment of the anointing of the queen is to take place under a golden canopy, "to shield Her Majesty from view during the most sacred of the coronation rituals," says one of the characters.[1] This is the moment when divine and human power collide, a mythology so deep and powerful that its connection must be wrapped in silence, secrecy, and mystery.

"Now we come to the anointing," says the Duke of Windsor to a party of close friends in his home watching the televised occasion and bitterly observing from afar. "The simple, most holy, most solemn, most sacred moment of the entire service."

"So how come we don't get to see it," an anonymous friend asks, as the screen of the TV goes blank and the young queen-to-be walks beneath the golden canopy.

---

1. Martin, "Smoke and Mirrors," 44:32.

THE MYTHOLOGY OF THE RICH RULING CLASS

"Because we are mortals," says the Duke of Windsor.[2]

I can't speak for the overarching artistic vision of those writers, producers, and director of *The Crown*, but my hunch is that they understood that twenty-first-century viewers might have a hard time swallowing the notion of the sacrosanctity of this moment of anointment, if not the blatant royal propaganda on demonstration. (Perhaps viewers of Charles III's ascent in 2023 had a similar experience of that coronation service, though *The Crown* serves as a vivid example through the dramatized tension between church officials and the public desire for information it portrays). The idea that God would ordain the members of a particularly wealthy family to the English crown, having witnessed the brutal legacy of that same crown in generations of colonization efforts over the previous centuries, is likely to strike some viewers as ludicrous. Yet, as strange as it might seem to some, the mythology that the divine author of creation ordains certain rulers is not an invention of the English monarchy under Elizabeth II, her father George VI, the abdicated Duke of Windsor, or her son Charles III, nor is it particular to monarchy.

It is a mythology because it establishes a pretext through which some persons rule over others by way of a set of unexamined relationships which are taken to be a given, particularly the magnetic relationship between wealth and ruling power. This mythology promotes the idea that wealth and ruling power are signs of divine favor or proof of human excellence, or both ideas at once. While it is difficult to prove divine favor or human excellence, the mythology relies on exactly what *The Crown's* "Smoke and Mirrors" episode demonstrates, that such events must take place out of sight of everyday persons precisely because to view them in the light of reason is to notice their pure fallibility. This chapter examines that mythology in some of its forms, identifying it as another problem against which ptoxocracy hopes to push. Taken as a given, the mythology of the rich ruling class serves as one of the primary mechanisms by which the poor are forgotten.

THE MYTHOLOGY OF RULE BY DIVINE AUTHORITY

One would expect that the sacred texts of those who have claimed rule by divine authority, say, within the Christian tradition, would be filled with pages of stories of divine authorization for kings and emperors. Yet what we find in the Old Testament is quite the opposite. Instead of stories of divine

2. Martin, "Smoke and Mirrors," 44:59.

excitement for kingly authority, we find divine reluctance, frustration, and anger.

The books of 1 and 2 Samuel in the Hebrew Bible tell a story of the people aching for monarchy despite warnings from God that it will rip them apart. In the early pages of the books, all the leaders of Israel gather, having known the wisdom of the prophet Samuel firsthand, but watching it perverted by his sons. The people are unsatisfied with the status quo of regional judges and local officials, and they wish to be more like their powerful neighbors. "Then all the elders of Israel gathered together and came to Samuel at Ramah and said to him, 'You are old, and your sons do not follow in your ways; appoint for us, then, a king to govern us, like other nations'" (1 Sam 8:4–5). Here we see the allure of the mythology of the wealthy ruling class: the people of God desire a rule of government that mirrors the methods of their pagan neighbors. Since these gentile neighbors all have kings, that's what the people want. Yet God warns the people of the dangers of divinely ordained kings:

> [God] said, "These will be the ways of the king who will reign over you: he will take your sons and appoint them to his chariots and to be his horsemen, and to run before his chariots, and he will appoint for himself commanders of thousands and commanders of fifties and some to plow his ground and to reap his harvest and to make his implements of war and the equipment of his chariots. He will take your daughters to be perfumers and cooks and bakers. He will take the best of your fields and vineyards and olive orchards and give them to his courtiers. He will take one-tenth of your grain and of your vineyards and give it to his officers and his courtiers. He will take your male and female slaves and the best of your cattle and donkeys and put them to his work." (1 Sam 8:11–17)

God warns the people that a divinely ordained ruler will use their power not only in the ways that they desire (going to war, defending the territory, becoming mighty), but also to oppress and make themselves wealthy at the expense of the people. This passage serves as a simple template for condemnation of the mythology of the wealthy ruling class found in the rest of this chapter: they will use power to enrich themselves further at the expense of the people whom they are called to serve. The ruler's authority will extend into all facets of life, including use of sons, daughters, land, possessions, home, and the fruits of one's labor. The connection between power and wealth, in other words, is inescapable. Wealth begets power, and power craves wealth. The people are warned by God not to let their desire for order lead them to such folly, but they do not listen.

Fast forwarding through the story, the people persist in their begging for a king and God finally relents. By way of the prophet Samuel, King Saul is hand-selected by God and anointed for service. Listen, however, to the reluctance of God as the new king is anointed for divinely authorized governance:

> Samuel summoned the people to the Lord at Mizpah and said to the Israelites, "Thus says the Lord, the God of Israel, 'I brought up Israel out of Egypt, and I rescued you from the hand of the Egyptians and from the hand of all the kingdoms that were oppressing you.' But today you have rejected your God, who saves you from all your calamities and your distresses, and you have said, 'No, but set a king over us.'" (1 Sam 10:17–19a)

God is greatly displeased at having been twisted into submission, knowing full well that a king will only bring more problems to the people. King Saul proves to be an awful ruler, the very embodiment of crass perversion of wealth and power that God had warned the people about earlier in the story. Saul will absolutely fulfill the words previously spoken.

Later, things get so bad with Saul that God commands that the prophet go behind the newly ordained king's back and select his successor, David. Righteous, though troubled at times, the Davidic monarchy eventually becomes the measure against which all other monarchs are gauged, a model for ruling class sanctity ordained by God and destiny. David is everything Saul is not, though he still manages to fall prey to the trappings of wealth and power. His son, Solomon, will be both wise and extremely wealthy, yet even under wise King Solomon, the nation splinters and fades, never to be the same after father and son leave power. Nevertheless, future rulers will be compared, to some extent, to David and Solomon.

The Davidic monarchy isn't the only tradition to give rise to a mythology whereby the ruling class and divinity are expressly mixed. One of the first acts of Octavian upon his ascent to the heights of Roman power as Emperor (44 BC), having cast down Marc Anthony and his enemies, was to put forward a motion in the Senate that Julius Caesar be considered a god. A cult would rise, and emperors who followed Octavian (known later as the Divine Augustus, after his death), would receive similar treatment. The connection to a divine ordination for power most obviously points to a source of authority. It will become the answer to a natural question of anyone who finds themselves subject. By what right does one person rule over another? The answer that arises out of these stories is obvious: by divine right, divine purpose, divine ordination. One can hardly conceive of a more powerful source of earthly authority than heavenly powers. David is anointed, while Augustus is raised to deity through senatorial debate and vote, though the effect is identical. As the duke says of the coronation of his niece in *The Crown*, onlookers are unable to watch her anointing because "we are mortal." The soon-to-be-queen, by extension, is not.

Perhaps it is a cynical thing, then, to point out that either these rulers ascended into power as some of the most extremely wealthy persons of their day or died among the wealthiest classes. King David is an example of the faithful, enlightened king, whose humble origins serve to bolster his sincerity and capacity as king. The story of a young shepherd, weakest and smallest of his brothers, destined by God to give rise to a legacy of authority, is a profound one of rags to riches indeed. Lest we forget this is the same child who slew Goliath, in the end even David's monarchy resembles that which God warned the people of before electing Saul in chapter 8: David raises armies by way of the sons of the nation, rapes the wife of a particularly faithful subject, goes to war endlessly, uses his position to entrench his own family's interests, and expresses political capital for his own personal gains. David's monarchy would be truly novel had King David resisted the temptation of wealth and proven God wrong about kings, but in the end, he founds a dynasty that—though splintered—will last for centuries and is immediately taken up by his son Solomon. David proves to be exactly the kind of king that God warned the people about through Samuel as it turns out, insofar as he employs his kingly authority in order to build his riches.

David's story, then, lends complicated credibility to the mythology of the wealthy ruler. Yes, he began poor and small (as his later apologists would absolutely have lifted as evidence of God's anointment), but in the end this divine blessing made him a very wealthy man. In a way, we might not be blamed for believing the blessing of God into ruling class authority made wealth a logical conclusion. How else will a king raise and pay armies to fulfill the divine mandate to rule without wealth? Taxes must be raised, and it only follows that a portion of these taxes must go to help the good and godly king appear as grand as the neighboring kingdoms. No matter how humble his beginnings, divinely authorized rulership would almost always lead to wealth. This, I believe, is part of the mythology of wealthy rulers: a ruler must have means to rule, so the two must necessarily be interlinked. Since God ordained this person to rule, this person must also be rich.

Democracies are just as susceptible to a mythology of the ruling class and its connection to divine authority, though some expressions of this mythology are more conspicuous than others. On the day he was elected Speaker of the House following weeks of rancor in the House of Representatives in 2023, newly elected leader Mike Johnson cited divine authorization out of his faith as a source of authority. "The Bible" he said, "is very clear that God is the one that raises up those in authority. He raised up each of you, all of us. And I believe that God has ordained and allowed each one of us to be brought here for this specific moment."[3] In claiming as much, Johnson demonstrated his capacity to engage an age-old idea of divinity as a source of authority in his own leadership. Much as we witnessed in the previous chapter, this kind of statement entails that the actions of those members of Congress briefed on the upcoming pandemic in 2019 and using that knowledge for their own financial gain, for instance, are not only actions that can be shielded from consequence by law, but they can be understood as authorized by divine right.

The power of the mythology of divinely authorized rich rulers is relatively simple. By telling a story in which power and wealth are inevitable copartners in ordained authority, be it through democratic, totalitarian, or monarchical mechanisms, this mythology blocks any possibility by which wealth and power are not inevitable outcomes of one another. Those daring to wonder aloud just who it is repeating the mythology, and what they seek to gain through it, are shushed by religious officials who represent the authority of such a divine story. Like any good mythology it both explains the way things are, reminds us of the inevitability of the present condition, and determines how things will—or should—unfold.

THE MYTHOLOGY OF MERITOCRACY

In the words of Matthew Desmond, "for as long as there has been poverty alongside great wealth, the winners have cultivated rationalizations for that arrangement."[4] This is the mythology of meritocracy. This mythology, as we receive it, begins with the imagination of the world as a logical place. Good is rewarded and evil is punished. If someone is rich or powerful, they have

---

3. Edmonson, "House Elects Mike Johnson," para. 9.
4. Desmond, *Poverty, by America*, 100.

earned or deserved it by virtue of their capacity. By extension, if someone is poor, they have earned or deserved it. This is the God-helps-those-who-help-themselves theory of wealth and poverty. It is a theology insofar as it explains characteristics of God's engagement with humankind, a manifestation of divine will, whether condemnatory or rewarding, and it is a mythology insofar as it explains the way things are as we encounter them. In the meritocratic mythology, God has blessed the rich with intelligence and skill and cursed the poor as unworthy and stupid. The rich, according to this mythology, deserve their wealth through the use of these gifts. The poor deserve their lot: they have been lazy or ineffective. Economic status is an absolute sign of deservedness, and never a product of manipulation or chance. Coupled with the myth of divine ruling right, wealth is thus a stamp of divine approval, the logical outcome of one's capacity.

Meritocracy is a mythological means of justifying things as they are rather than an honest description of the way things function. If meritocracy were real, for example, then the most intelligent persons would get the highest paid jobs, the most important promotions, and the best slots in the most elite schools. One would expect that the most talented persons would receive the best treatment if the mythology were true. Yet recent studies reveal the way in which legacy admissions at Ivy League schools disproportionately entitle wealthy individuals to such an education, and the ways that high SAT scores correlate directly to relative wealth of families rather than actual academic capacity.[5] One particular study showed that wealthy students are no likelier to succeed at these schools and essentially that merit-based admission criteria are a fallacy. These studies demonstrate the ways that wealth, not skill or intelligence, becomes the determining factor in whether one has access to a system of self-betterment.[6] When that happens, we end up with a system-wide feedback loop. The rich get richer, and the poor continue to get left out, however meritorious their accomplishments or potential.

Former Fortune 100 executive and businessman Thomas Vozzo reflects on the mythology of meritocracy in his own life, and the ways he has witnessed its shortcomings in his time as CEO of Homeboy Industries. He writes, "In the Forgotten America, that of the poor and disenfranchised, [the poor] have almost no chance in a merit-based system, and there is no level playing field. They have so many cultural and societal barriers that

---

5. Bhatia et al., "Study of Elite College."
6. Chetty et al., "Diversifying Society's Leaders."

prevent them from even being able to play the game."[7] He attests that this mythology would seem validated by the fact of his own story, that of a child of working-class parents who lifts himself into the highest rungs of corporate power structures through his own skill. Yet as Homeboy's CEO, Vozzo's self-interpretation quickly vanished. He writes, "I saw several examples" at Homeboy "that tangibly challenged me to think differently about meritocracy. We had several managers who, if they were from the side of the tracks I was from, would be zooming up the ladder of success. But because they were not, life doesn't work out that way for them."[8] Meritocracy fails the poor because its outcomes are available only to a sliver of society. Vozzo cites Martin Luther King Jr., who once said in an interview, "I believe we ought to do all we can and seek to lift ourselves by our own bootstraps, but it is a cruel jest to say to a bootless man that he ought to lift himself up by his own bootstraps."[9]

Not only is meritocracy a fallacious promise to the poor, but it serves as a justification to the wealthy as the basis of their wealth. In this way the mythology of meritocracy serves as a device by which the wealthy become myopic. By determining their own economic station in life as founded upon their merit, they discover the justification for disdain of those who are not wealthy. These two mythologies—that is, the mythology of rule by divine right and the meritocratic mythology—form the basis of the mythology of the rich ruling class.

Their potency lies in the unrelenting insistence that wealth and ruling power are not only corollaries, but *deservingly* so. The arrangement, as Desmond suggests, is a fabrication and rationalization of a phenomenon, and never the other way around. The mythology of a wealthy ruling class is an intentional invention of power-brokers determined to hold on to power as long as they can: by making wealth and power necessary corollaries of one another there is no possibility through which anyone else might justifiably rule. In becoming necessary corollaries, they take on the potential as currencies of exchange in the economies of one another.

---

7. Vozzo, *Homeboy Way*, 179.
8. Vozzo, *Homeboy Way*, 99.
9. King, "11 Months Before," 16:48.

THE GIVENNESS OF WEALTH AND POWER

An idea is sometimes at its most dangerous when it accomplishes *givenness*. In philosophical circles one might call this an *a priori* argument (that is, a presupposition rather than a conclusion), but for the sake of simplicity we will continue using the word *given* here. Givenness isn't always a bad thing. Sometimes we take certain things for granted because they help us move through the world less burdened, and other times our snap judgments based on givens lead to baseless conclusions.

As a pastor some of my most humorous moments in ministry come when strangers, community members, or parishioners make assumptions about how I might act or judge them given the fact that I wear symbols associated with the clergy in public places. I remember the first time, for example, that I experienced the givenness of my position while in divinity school. I happened to be walking to a funeral at the church where I was a pastoral education student; I was wearing my clerical collar. The building sits just down the block from Wrigley Field in Chicago, a hot spot for Saturday parties, especially on this St. Paddy's Day weekend. Parking was terrible. I found a spot several blocks away from the church and proceeded to walk the half mile or so in my collar and black suit. It was about nine o'clock in the morning, but down the road I spotted a group of young men about my age, hands filled with red plastic cups and cigarettes. As I neared them each of the young men squared up and stood to the side. "Father," each said, in turn, holding their cigarettes behind their backs and looking shamefully at the ground as I passed between them on the sidewalk. It was a given for them, apparently, that someone dressed in black and wearing a clerical collar should be judging their behavior with scorn. Little did they know, were it not for the funeral I might have been joining them on that beautiful spring morning!

Examples abound of assumptions and biases leading us astray, but again, there is no reason to believe that givenness should be a bad thing altogether. Sometimes our assumptions and learned experiences are helpful. Yet the given relationship of wealth and power is a more unhelpful set of assumptions. The given connection between wealth and power to which we now turn is that way in which it is taken that wealth ought to be allowed to be translated into political power, that wealth and political power are interchangeable currencies.

The translation of material purchasing power into political power is not a societal evil in and of itself. Certainly, there are those who have used their wealth to express themselves toward the ends of equality, justice, and peacemaking. Numerous examples exist of kindhearted people influencing politics for the better from the authority of their purchasing power. Those who provided bail-bond money during the civil rights movement translated their wealth into liberation for the unjustly imprisoned, for example. Likewise, a serene piece of property known as Torrey Pines State Natural Reserve in the city of San Diego would have otherwise been gobbled up as prime real estate for developers had it not been preserved by just such a wealthy benefactor. There is no doubt that some wealthy persons have used their power for good in the world and completely refused their political purchasing power. Whether wealth can be used for moral ends is not the subject of this discussion. It absolutely can be used toward moral good. I can attest to this firsthand: many wealthy people contribute to the ministries of my church, which I believe are doing incredible good in the world, and which we would not be capable of offering if it weren't for their dollars.

What is worth examining, rather, is that tendency of wealth to dominate political discourse and policy making over and above all other factors, that wealth can be translated into an unaccountable source of political power. What is at hand is the givenness of the entitlement of the wealthy to political purchasing power, and whether the potential for political purchasing power is a societal good in and of itself, or whether a society might consider regulating this magnetic connection to some extent. The wealthy can translate the purchasing power of their material goods into political ends in ways that those without wealth cannot. They do this in legal ways, like donating to campaigns and purchasing advertising spots for those running for elected office and can also do it in illegal ways like bribing officials. The wealthy hold more potential political power than poor citizens.

There is an argument here, I should note, that the wealthy hold a certain perspective that is more valuable to society at large than a poor person. Fascinatingly, land ownership was one of the primary criteria for eligibility of officeholders in periods of the ancient Roman Republic. One had to prove status of material wealth to be eligible for elected office or to place a vote in the forum. In a generous read of the idea that society might impose a condition of wealth as an eligibility requirement for governance, one might argue that the rich must have a stake in government because their material goods are most impacted by state policies. By this argument, the rich have a vested interest in good governance because good governance is good for business, and what is good for business is good for society. A just society is one (assuming democratic norms) in which governance frees the individual to pursue their interests.

Whether one can agree that historical evidence has validated these claims is yet to be determined. On the one hand, we generally believe that a society functions well when its enterprises are allowed room for creativity and curiosity, and that a state that cannot bear to allow these is one doomed to eventual failure. On the other hand, chattel slavery was a profitable business for those Americans who invested in it before the American Civil War and whose shareholders lobbied hard for its maintenance in society. Morally repugnant as it was, no one could argue that it was not a good investment insofar as it provided a steady stream of returns for these stakeholders. In fact, one could argue that chattel slavery was so good for business in the mid-nineteenth century that an entire nation was forced to decide the question over arms, that the presence of so much potential through wealth creation is the very basis by which wealthy interests were driven to violent means of protection. In other words, good business does not necessarily translate into a moral society—in fact, it may do the opposite.

But again, to return to the question. Ought it be a given that wealth should so easily translate into political power? It is certainly true that wealth can be either a good force or a bad force in politics. The question of givenness remains uncertain.

The same question can be asked of politics and ruling-class decision-making. As we have seen already in the previous chapter, as it turns out, the rich tend to express their power politically in ways that ostracize and forget the interests of anyone except the rich. Again, the question is not whether wealth can influence politics or whether it can influence it for better or worse, but to challenge the assumption that the wealthy should have any more influence over decision-making and policy capacities than anyone else simply because of their wealth. This is the givenness of wealth and power that is addressed here.

Whether one earns or inherits their wealth makes even less of a difference. In a sense, one can imagine that someone who has recently earned their own wealth and entered the world of the rich might be an excellent decision-maker, whereas one who inherits their wealth simply did the work of being born. But this argument shows the ways that we assume that the business of statecraft and the business of wealth-creation are the same.

Again, instead of demonstrating a counterexample, it merely illuminates the ways in which we take wealth to be the measure of all good things. If this were true, then the wealthiest citizen should also be the best spiritual leader, best golf player, and best skateboarder. Of course, the newly minted wealthy person possesses a certain skill set that translates into the possible generation of wealth, but does that skill set entitle them to a position of policy making? No. The rich are no more suited to the work of statecraft than the world's most talented skateboarder is entitled to hold public office. Just because a person is skilled at one thing doesn't mean—that is, it isn't a given—that they'll be good at another thing. While the mythology of the wealthy ruler entices us to believe that the rich make good rulers, history asserts the opposite: the wealthy are particularly ill-suited for public office insofar as they lack a stake in the lives of the poor. Lacking a stake in the lives of the poor, they lack a stake in the good of society at large.

Poking and prodding about, one becomes curious as to how wealth and political purchasing power became so intimately intertwined, how the givenness of one begetting another might have arisen. Clergy like me have long stoked moralistic and judgmental personas in public, especially those who continue to wear black and dress in a collar on Saturday mornings. I have little wonder as to how those young men in Chicago hid their cigarettes and cups of beer from me, as such is the accomplishment of my predecessors in crafting an image of pastor as moral policeman! It was not by accident or divine intervention that they chose to hide, it was learned behavior based on intentional identity-shaping decisions. One must wonder how and whether the connection between wealth and political purchasing power ought to be a given, but more curiously, who is responsible for that connection. Did we learn this from natural experience, or were we taught this intentionally? The mere prodding of that question unsettles givenness, which I would argue is a societal good in and of itself. In other words, the mythology of the wealthy ruling class is a story told by the rich for the sake of the rich, that they may freely exchange wealth for power, and power for wealth. It is a given invention, not a necessary and logical end.

The danger here is that when we take the mythology of the rich ruling class and couple it with the given assumption that wealth ought to be able to purchase as much political power as it deems necessary (without check or balance), we arrive at a completely lopsided social reality, one in which the rich are fully justified in all their decisions, no matter the effect on the lives of the poor. This, it seems, is the most dangerous implication of the mythology of the rich ruling class and the given that wealth ought to purchase political power: by assenting to its precepts, by establishing wealth and power as coexistent inevitabilities of one another, the rich insulate themselves. If their authority is ultimately derivative of or leading toward wealth, then why should they have a stake in the poor? What good is a stake in the poor when power and wealth are foregone conclusions? The mythology of the rich ruling class says that wealth forms not only a given connection to political power, but that the rich are deserving of this power, as evidenced by the fact of their wealth.

DANGEROUS MYTHOLOGIES

It is here, then, that we can begin to unravel the mystery behind the mythology and plot a way forward. Part of undoing the mythology of the wealthy ruling class begins with asserting that there is nothing particularly special about wealthy individuals except their wealth and the capacity of that very wealth as political purchasing power—that is to say that in fact, while wealth may be a sign of virtue (as in a very intelligent person earning a MacArthur "genius" grant) it is not necessarily so. To be sure, great leadership does not come naturally to everyone. There is just as high a proportion of under-qualified leaders from the middle and lower classes as there is among the rich. Again, it is of no benefit to valorize or idealize the poor, and one must be careful here to equalize potential rather than draw from exceptionality of class as a means of justification; the poor are no more innately well-suited to leadership than the rich. Economic status, therefore, is not an indication of natural giftedness toward handling political power. Meritocracy is a fallacy because it cannot prove itself in either direction. The difference is that bad rulers from the highest class have the means to convince others, by way of honest or dishonest means, that they are deserving of power, blessed for it, or ordained for it. The middle class have a few more ways of gaining attraction through professional means and the few possibilities that meritocracy might enable, while the poor are almost always locked out of political authority, no matter their capacity. There are a few examples to the contrary, to be certain. Yet the danger of the mythology of the rich ruling class serves as a mechanism which both validates certain persons for governance and invalidates others. Wealth, in other words, becomes a prerequisite for power. It is here that we find both the tragedy and injustice of this mythology.

THE MYTHOLOGY OF THE RICH RULING CLASS

One might choose to argue against this problem by pointing toward numerous revolutions and toppled governments that achieved political power not by way of wealth but by force. In the case of revolution-era Cuba, for example, there is no doubt of communism's appeal to the working class and poor people. The abuse of the poor at the hands of the wealthy ruling classes in mid-century Cuba prior to Fidel Castro's landing the yacht *Granma* on its shores is well documented. Batista's fall from Cuban political power has as much to do with the revolutionary's tactic capacity as it does with the abuses of his regime, and the ways that democratic colonizing wealthy interests in the United States and Europe supported him so eagerly. One might argue that the revolutionary path from poor to ruling class authority finally undoes the mythology of wealth and power, that the poor are able to gain ruling authority by way of revolution. So long as the poor have a viable pathway toward power (violent as it is), the mythology becomes less potent, and therefore ultimately fails.

Yet two things can be said of this. First, one might examine closely the revolutionary leaders who emerge in power vacuums like Cuba. While Ché Guevara, it might be said, was the true embodiment of the Davidic rags-to-power story, Fidel Castro was not. Castro was born to a land-owning family, while Guevara holds a special place in the hearts of Cubans to this day for his humble origins and solidarity with the poor. Nevertheless, even though Guevara didn't survive the revolution (not long enough to know whether he would end up wealthy, that is), we do know the outcome of the Castro regime. (Much to the fascination of conspiracy theorists the pure-of-heart Guevara didn't make his way to the end of the revolution alive and therefore is hard to pin down in either direction). To this day, despite communist ideology, the Castros remain among the wealthiest families in Cuba. In fact, while the people of Cuba suffer, the Castros maintain a lifestyle that well exceeds that of their neighbors, only serving to double the evidence for a mythology of wealth and power.

Fidel Castro and King David would seem to have this in common, then, that wealth becomes a necessary conclusion of power. The revolutionary must become the aristocrat. This is his burden to bear. Though he forsakes his ideology in doing so, it is a sacrifice he makes willingly, even eagerly. In the end, the temptation of exchanging wealth for power, and power for wealth, are too great for even the purest-hearted revolutionaries. Because these two—wealth and power—are a given interchangeable as currency, systemic economic changes will not and cannot lead to the betterment of the poor unless the connection between these two is severed.

Revolutions are costly enterprises when the human life hangs upon the scale, which cost lives, time, and productivity, as well as cultural and social goods. These costs are born most especially by the poor. For one to argue against the existence of a mythology of wealth and power as inevitable partners based on the possibility of revolution, one has already declared this mythology a dominant reality. Revolution is the means of last resort, a desperation of the poor when the rich will not heed their calls, not something to be desired or used at a whim, for it will likely cause disaster to the poor. Its existence points to a failure of governance, not a possible path to be emulated or striven toward. A revolutionary path for the poor becomes inevitable when it becomes clear that the wealthy have so little stake in the lives of the poor that absolutely nothing can be done to beg otherwise. By forgetting the poor, by shielding themselves from the realities of poor people, the rich, in fact, become bad rulers. This is as true of the ancien régime of prerevolutionary France as it is of Fidel Castro: wealthy leaders become ill-suited for a task that calls upon them to serve the interests of the whole precisely by virtue of their wealth and the disconnection it yields.

This, it seems, is the most dangerous implication of the mythology of the rich ruling class. By assenting to its precepts, by establishing wealth and power as coexistent inevitabilities of one another, the rich insulate themselves from questionability; thus they insulate themselves from a meaningful stake in the lives of the poor. What good is a stake in the poor when power and wealth are foregone conclusions?

Finally, the problem of wealth in ruling-class interests goes beyond the disinterestedness in the poor. If wealth and power cling to one another, the effect of their magnetism is concentration and isolation. The needs of others are cast out at the expense of the magnitude of the new thing birthed at the hands of wealth and power. This new creation yields rulers who are cut off from their subjects, a thing no less possible in democracy than in monarchy or any other form of governance. They hide out in private lounges, eat fine foods in small restaurants serviced by hushed workers sworn to secrecy by nondisclosure agreements, and hold meetings with other isolated rulers whose children go to fine schools. Myopia and isolation do not naturally relent when tempted by the security they bring. This is, in fact, exactly what it would seem to mean to be a bad ruler in any sense of the word.

To this point one might say that until now we have spoken much of totalitarians and monarchs, but little of democracy. Yet it is here that this mythology is most dangerous, for it hides blamelessly behind equality, even as the mythology of democracy as a great equalizing force is also undone by the rich. Yes, the poor have an equal vote in electing officials (though in some US states one could argue that incarceration, a reduction in polling locations, and a return to in-hand proof of identity are penalizations of poverty, and thus a way for the rich to control the voting capacities of the poor), but they are not equally capable for standing for election. Elections are expensive and require deep pockets. One must either hold funds themselves or fundraise, and fundraising is best done through connections to the wealthy. Here again the wealthy control the levers of democracy, in vetting and disabling candidates before they ever have the potential to run for election through the expression (or withholding) of their wealth. One has the impression that in this way the rich, whether they stand for election as rulers themselves, are the gatekeepers of democracy.

In his work *Politics* Aristotle writes, "Democracy is the rule of the poor; oligarchy is that of the rich."[10] While Aristotle suggests that democracy will necessarily endow the poor with more power than the rich within a democracy, history has demonstrated that Aristotle underestimates the exchange of power for wealth within democracy, of the power of the rich to dominate the poor through the domineering translation of wealth into political power. The rich are equally if not more capable of exerting power upon the poor within democracy, using the mechanism of democracy as a means of hiding their actions. Thanks to a lack of campaign finance laws and regulations in the United States, and much intentional undoing of safeguards of those laws by the Supreme Court, for example, one can scarcely find a counterargument to this claim except in a few exceptional cases. Thus, by the very mechanisms of democracy itself, the capacity of democracy to allow equitable treatment as citizen decision-makers is undone by the rich. Contrary to Aristotle's fear that democracy entails rule by the poor, the mechanisms of democracy continue to allow for rule by the rich because of the translation of wealth into political power.

Not only does the mythology of the rich ruling class lead us to believe that rich rulers, as such, deserve their power, but it will also have us believe that the interests of the ruling class and the interests of the many are one and the same, that whatever is good for the rulers is good for the people.

10. Aristotle, *Politics*, 37.

History has shown otherwise time and time again, and yet this idea is reincarnated every generation by one name or another. In some generations it is named *trickle-down economics*, in others *feudal lordship*. The idea is nothing more than a necessary mythology propagated by the wealthy to maintain both wealth and political strength. Mythologies like this are powerful because, like Queen Elizabeth II's golden coronation canopy, they shield the rich from accountability, urging the viewer to imbue the action under the golden canopy as unfitting for the eyes of mere mortals.

I call this the *mythology of the rich ruling class* because there is a mythology at work in society that imagines that becoming a ruler automatically bestows one with a sense of responsibility for the good of one's people, that automatically in stepping into power the ruling class somehow becomes disentangled from their own interests and begins seeing the interests of others more fully. True, some wealthy officials absolutely consider the needs and well-being of the poor, and their own wealth enables them to comprehend complex problems because they have dealt in complex matters as a wealthy person. The argument until now has not been that the rich are incapable of seeking anything good for anyone but the rich. Charity may, in fact, be well-intentioned. But the mythology of the rich ruling class is dangerous because it leads us to believe that rulers have a given commitment to the well-being of all citizens, and this is most certainly an exceptional claim. Some rulers may believe that the well-being of all citizens is a high good, but this is a very different thing than saying that the rich have an interest in the poor, or a stake in the outcome of their lives.

CONCLUSION

The time has come to conceive of a new system of governance whereby the marriage of wealth and power might be decoupled. Problems of this mythology include the unfair advantage of the wealthy in the democratic process, the antidemocratic tendencies of the wealthy, the tendencies of the wealthy to employ governmental processes and systems for their own personal gain, the incapacity of the wealthy to demonstrate a historical excellence in governing, wealth concentration aided by power concentration, and most of all, the absence of the interest in the well-being of the materially poor. It is the last problem that is the most dubious of traits of rich rulers: the rich have no reason to care for the poor. They have reason to use and abuse, to exploit, to be charitable toward the poor (depending on their belief or moral system), but they do not have an interest in the poor. It is the lack of a stake in the lives of the poor that, I argue, renders them not only bad rulers, but ultimately incapable of good governance.

So it is here that we come to a new horizon, a new imagination for a system that provides an actual stake in the lives of the poor: ptoxocracy, or rule by the abject poor. Ptoxocracy originates where the challenge is fiercest to sever the seemingly inviolable connection between wealth and power in a nonviolent manner. Ptoxocracy is the thesis of this project, but it is a genuine contribution to democratic republicanism that emerges from within the heart of the Christian tradition, the end toward which the title points. The end toward which we point is the fulfillment of the psalmist's cry, that the poor are not forgotten. It is an attempt to imagine a plausible future in which the rich hold a meaningful stake in the lives of the *ptoxoi*.

3

Ptoxocracy

Governance by the materially poor; a hybrid form of representative democracy whereby only persons of the lowest economic status are eligible for elected public office

WE CANNOT NOT RELY on wishful thinking or high-minded moralistic principles alone to do the work of justice. We must create a possible system of governance that takes the moral shortcomings of human actions seriously. Most precisely, such a system must take account of the amnesia of the rich toward the poor, what in Christian terms we might describe as their primary sin against the poor. What I'm trying to avoid is the kind of thinking that leads to statements like, "I wish we could all just be better people," or even, "If people had more education (or better education, or the right kind of education, or the right kinds of political beliefs) the world would be a better place." I'm not convinced by those sentiments, because both "better people" and "more/better/right education" are subjective ideas. Those whose ideas I find morally reprehensible might just as easily make such statements about me. What we need is a structure that gives the rich some kind of meaningful stake in the lives of the poor without relying on ethical norms like charity. We must imagine a possible future in which the eradication of the great chasm between rich and poor is bridged not by grandiose rhetoric or hopes for higher morality of the rich, but a bridge made of lasting structural material.

The rich have proven themselves incapable of living beyond a mythology which imbues their lives with more importance than the poor, such that we must imagine a possible future beyond the power of the myth. Imagining possible futures is something we do all the time, from the menial tasks of everyday life to the larger projects that constitute our vocation. As I write this, for example, it's near the end of the day, I'm feeling tired and it's almost time to pick up my child from school. I have possible futures ahead of me. I can decide to push through the weariness, making a cup of coffee in hopes that I'll be more awake when I return to the computer. That possible future requires a phone call to my spouse, asking that she pick up our child, a possibility that raises the potential of some future ire in my direction. I could also save this document and shut down my computer, following through on an earlier promise to pick up my child. A third idea comes to me, though: maybe I'll do neither. I'll keep pushing through my exhaustion, neither calling my wife nor making coffee nor closing my document, hoping beyond hope that a mad dash toward the finish line will help me construct a timeless work of theology over the next few hours. Given that the third possibility would damage trust with my spouse (or leave me sleeping on the couch tonight), and knowing that meaningful works of theology take time, hard work, months of good nights of rest, and thoughtfulness (and knowing that great works of theology are just hard to create in the first place), I don't believe that the third option exists as a possible future. The first and second futures are possible, though if I'm honest, only one is plausible.

That's the kind of system ptoxocracy aims to become: a possible future that does not require wishful, unrealistic thinking, however lofty or beautiful that wishful thinking might be. Overreliance on wishful thinking has failed the poor, and it is time we engage our imaginative capacity for possible futures.

IMAGINATION BEYOND BIAS

Systems theorist Edwin Friedman, writing of the inherent riskiness and reward of imagining possible futures, writes, "In order to imagine the unimaginable, people must be able to separate themselves from surrounding emotional processes before they can even begin to see (or hear) things differently."[1] Because wealth and finances are so intrinsically connected to

---

1. Friedman, *Failure of Nerve*, 31.

our senses of well-being, security, and self-worth, one challenge we must push through in order to explore ptoxocracy is those "emotional processes" we rely upon to move through the world on a daily basis—namely, our biases. To proceed into the substance of ptoxocracy as a possible future we must first take stock of our biases to dispel some of their aura of infallibility. Usually biases against the poor take the form of a righteous or moral belief in meritocracy, that the poor exist as such in their state because of individual choices they've made. Some of us may have direct experiences with *ptoxoi* and can attempt to generalize on hygiene, demeanor, intelligence, or capacity to communicate effectively. These biases may even hold some truth, just as in many cases they do not. This is nothing to say of the biases that the poor hold against themselves, given the relentlessness of narratives that constantly belittle their dignity and self-worth. Greg Boyle reminds readers of the devastation that such self-perception can inflict in communities, writing that "in the high poverty urban communities of Los Angeles County, one in three youth suffers from post-traumatic stress disorder. That's twice the rate of soldiers returning from war."[2] Biases blind us from these kinds of facts.

Biases are a shorthand for navigating reality in a hurry, though we need not leave them unexamined. Sometimes they are helpful, and sometimes not. For example, there may be truth to a general set of biases against white, male, Protestant clergy as arrogant know-it-alls. I may even exhibit traces of these characteristics accidentally in my own behavior. Yet it does little to confirm reality: there are, of course, many white, male, Protestant clergy who are gentle, humble, and without a trace of arrogance in their actions. In other words, just because we can make snap judgments about a given group, and even if these judgments are based in experience, it does not make them universally true. It does, however, point to the existence of a bias, which I invite the reader to reflect upon and hold in gentle suspension as we explore the possible future of ptoxocracy. Doing this, we free ourselves from the nerve-wracking parameters of these biases so that we can explore possible futures with a sense of curiosity.

---

2. Boyle, *Barking to the Choir*, 56.

PTOXOCRACY

HOW TO CREATE A MEANINGFUL STAKE IN THE LIVES OF THE POOR

Decoupling Wealth and Political Power

If it is true that the rich have no meaningful stake in the lives of the poor, then our work is to create one. To begin exploring ptoxocracy we must begin with a few foundational assertions.

First: not all persons can or will become rich, but all persons are able to become poor. This is a relatively straightforward observation of economic reality. The foundation of ptoxocracy is the capacity of any person to either exist in or freely enter materially poor economic conditions. This seems to be exactly the kind of thing that Jesus has in mind, for example, when he calls the disciples into lives of poverty as his followers, to drop their nets and follow him. It's a much simpler task, a much more equitable one at least, than his asking for a buy-in fee. Had Jesus asked for up-front membership dues from his perspective followers at calling time, it's likely that he wouldn't have had many. Ptoxocracy takes this as a starting point for that which allows a citizen to enter social and political power. Despite the mythologies of self-betterment and meritocracy that tell us otherwise, it is not true: no evidence from history suggests that a poor person may become rich simply by willing it. Hard work and pulling ourselves up by the bootstraps do indeed occasionally yield wealth, yet hard-working people are no more likely to end up rich than lazy rich people are to end up poor. That is to say that most poor are not willfully poor. Given the realities of election economics, this means that the poor do not have equal opportunity for political power. Wealth, as we have seen, becomes a precondition to representative government and ruling power. The rich are no more qualified to rule than the poor, yet their economic status renders their ruling capacity something of an inevitability, which not only shuts out other decision-makers from power, it also means that the primary interests of the ruling class will always and only be the interests of the rich.

It is important here to note that ptoxocracy is understood to be a refinement of representative democracy, not a replacement. There may be other forms of ptoxocracy possible, but within this text ptoxocracy is understood to be a modification to the existing frame of representative democracy. To imagine a possible future that engages the realm of plausibility, we must seek to contain our hopes to what is at our disposal. As such, the first underlining axiom of ptoxocracy, that any person may be or become poor, is followed by an assertion of an explicitly ptoxocratic substance flowing from the axiom: within a ptoxocratic representative democracy, a person may be rich or may be powerful (in a representative, ruling political sense), but one may never be both.

Remembering that our aim is to create a possible future (not just an imaginary aim) clarifies why this ptoxocratic assertion follows the first. Is it possible to conceive of a society in which the rich willingly allow themselves to be ruled by the poor? Maybe, but it is certainly implausible without also imagining some kind of external force coercing them so. Our aim is to create a structure for a possible future that not only is helpful in remembering the poor, but that also conforms to general principles of justice, so that a possible future of the poor ruling over the rich feels quite implausible without the injection of a new variable in the equation. Wealth and political power are magnetic forces of historic coupling, such that it is implausible to imagine governance by the poor without their decoupling. The decoupling of power and wealth is the core aim of ptoxocracy, and this foremost assertion, following from a near axiomatic truth of one's willingness to enter poverty, achieves this cleanly. A system is ptoxocratic in nature if it accomplishes this task and is not ptoxocratic without it.

Importantly, nowhere within this assertion does one have to be poor, or consider the rich somehow morally abhorrent, or create a system that would seek to strip riches away from those who have achieved such wealth. Nowhere within the ptoxocratic assertion is a call for redistribution of wealth, or the moral superiority of poor persons. Moreover, nothing in ptoxocracy aims the system vindictively or retributively against the rich. This is one of the most constant failings of over-generalized understandings that emerge in every undergraduate introductory course of political science at every university. Novice students of Marxism, even those sympathetic to its project, almost constantly levy a critique that runs as follows: if we strip the rich of their wealth and give it to the poor, then what incentive do the rich have for working? Aren't we simply swapping one soon-to-be rich ruling class (aristocracy) for the old set of aristocrats? Marxism, it is then said, disincentives wealth, and therefore places society at risk of decay because it creates a disincentivizing downward spiral of economics.

Whether one holds these criticisms as valid is of no use or cost to ptoxocracy, yet one way to avoid decay of this nature is by decoupling wealth from power. Notice how the ptoxocratic assertion avoids the baseline critique of Marxism altogether by maintaining the possibility of wealth within society. It also maintains the possibilities of pluralistic society insofar as it does not require uniformity of moral beliefs, religious identity, or economics. A person in a ptoxocratic system may be as wealthy as they please and hold whatever beliefs constitute meaning in their lives, but their wealth does not entitle them to a share of political power; rather, it excludes them from it. Ptoxocracy is only possible if wealth is the very thing that cuts persons off from political power. The wealthy may continue to vote and voice opinion in the halls of power as any other citizen might, but the capacity of wealth to dictate the paths of justice and policy is shut down completely in ptoxocracy. The capacity to translate financial currencies into political ones is cut.

The Ptoxocratic Eligibility Requirement

Ptoxocratic representative democracy accomplishes the decoupling of power from wealth by way of a simple eligibility requirement: the only persons eligible for elected office are the *ptoxoi*. Now, eligibility requirements as civil protections for vulnerable persons are nothing extraordinary. Governments function in just such a way via the elimination of such exchanges all the time. Take alcohol consumption, which poses a particular danger to the healthy development of teenage brains. Given this danger, governments intervene via eligibility requirements to determine which persons may legally attain these goods, and those who may not. Society at large takes it as acceptable that eligibility restrictions may be placed on these, because we understand that certain persons' exposure to alcohol (namely, young developing minds) situates them at particular risk. Moreover, we also understand that alcohol is both culturally desired and highly addictive. Such an eligibility requirement helps us acknowledge, then, the dangers of alcohol to these brains, as well as the cultural norms informing their desire to imbibe.

In just such a way, ptoxocracy understands that the connection between wealth and power is just such a dangerous coupling. To have access to one of these (wealth or power) is an acceptable good for society, but to hold both is to engage the strong possibility for violence and injustice. Just as the stunting of brain development is not absolutely guaranteed by a minor's consumption of alcohol, neither is the marriage of wealth and power necessarily going to produce violence, yet it is an outcome that history bears out time and again. The seemingly inviolable connection between wealth and power (the mythology of the wealthy ruler) is exactly what ptoxocracy seeks to sever precisely because of this potential. When wealth and power are allowed to coexist without check or balance, the outcome is consistently and overwhelmingly negative for the poor, because the rich, as we have seen, have no meaningful stake in the lives of the poor. The constant coupling of wealth and power yields a lack in accountability, and to quote Stout again, "Power minus accountability equals domination."[3] Following Stout's equation as such, we might say that the magnetic connection between wealth and political power yields a lack of accountability for the wealthy, resulting in domination.

So, within representative democracy, ptoxocracy yields a simple control mechanism in the form of an eligibility requirement that follows from the first assertion, as well as the possibility that all human beings may become poor: in a ptoxocratic system, the only members of society eligible to stand for representative election are those who are materially poor. Since anyone can become poor, this means that power is theoretically available to more members of society (not already disqualified by other eligibility requirements) than without such an eligibility requirement.

To those who might object to the ptoxocratic insertion of such an eligibility requirement, we must recall that there is nothing particularly radical about placing eligibility requirements on civic officeholders. Society places eligibility limits on officeholders all the time. The US Constitution places limits on age for both the legislative and executive federal branches of government. Article II, section 1 of the US Constitution reads, "No Person except a natural born Citizen, or a Citizen of the United States, at the time of the Adoption of this Constitution, shall be eligible to the Office of President; neither shall any person be eligible to that Office who shall not have attained to the Age of thirty-five Years, and been fourteen Years a Resident within the United States."[4] In other words, the US Constitution's first section contains three important eligibility requirements for the office of president: natural citizenship, age, and minimum time of residence. Moreover, eligibility requirements aren't the sole restriction of the executive branch. In the case of the judicial branch, both federal and state judicial officeholders must have some kind of legal background and authority on which they may be appointed or elected. In the state of Washington, for example, to appear on a county ballot for the office of superior court, one

---

3. Stout, *Blessed Are the Organized*, 63.
4. US Const. art. II, § 1, cl. 5.

must have held residency in the district of their proposed candidacy for a minimum of one year, and have had a minimum of five years of admitted (qualified) law practice; that is, they must be a member in good standing with the local county bar association.

An eligibility requirement for officeholders based on the material wealth of a person accomplishes the severing of wealth and power, which is the aim of ptoxocracy. Under such a system, one may seek to be rich, or one may seek to become politically powerful, but never both at once. The one who seeks both must admittedly be compelled—by the usual mechanisms through which governments can peaceably exert authority over citizens—to choose either one or the other. Representative democracies accomplish exactly these sorts of things all the time through peaceful eligibility requirements with no need for coercion by force, taxation, penalty, or even punitive measures. We can say something similar of an age requirement, though it is not a usual way of framing such an eligibility requirement for office: in the United States of America, one may be thirty-four years old, and one may hold the office of US President, but one may not be both at once. Nothing in ptoxocracy suggests that one cannot be rich if one chooses to be at some point in their lives, but it does mean that choosing wealth is a choice against political power at a given moment.

This likely goes without saying, but ptoxocracy renders no eligibility requirement for voters. This is not an argument about suffrage. Even though suffrage has historically been based in economic terms, and universal suffrage is a relatively new addition to representative democracy, ptoxocracy makes no attempt to modify universal suffrage. Rendering the rich ineligible for office accomplishes ptoxocratic aims well before rescinding their right to vote, which is therefore both antidemocratic and unnecessary. It is an important distinction to note that the eligibility requirement of ptoxocracy would only affect those seeking to hold office, not voters in general. Ptoxocracy is a simple modification of accepted democratic norms that holds universal suffrage intact.

Implications of Ptoxocratic Eligibility Requirements

In his farewell address to the citizens of the United States, President Joseph Biden warned the nation of "the dangerous concentration of power in the hands of a very few ultrawealthy people, and the dangerous consequences if their abuse of power is left unchecked."[5] To hear these words from the mouths of progressive activists or social justice theorists would be one thing, but hearing them spoken from out of the Oval Office is historically exceptional. Clearly the relationship between the interests of the wealthy and their access to political power troubled Biden. He went on: "Today, an oligarchy is taking shape in America of extreme wealth, power and influence that literally threatens our entire democracy."[6]

Political, ruling-class power is like water: it will find the surest path downward. One might argue against ptoxocracy in noting that an eligibility requirement could only go so far in influencing the aims of the rich in exerting their political power, but that the rich will always find ways to exert purchasing power. Lobbyists that represent the interest of the wealthy on K Street are not elected officials, yet they exert tremendous force in US politics. Given the economics of elections that severely curtail the possibility of poor candidates in elected office, one's economic status is already an eligibility requirement for elected office in the United States, though that is hardly a good thing. Moreover, it creates a situation whereby those poor elected officials are indebted to their wealthy benefactors. This is possible, and a ptoxocratic system would indeed need to be a sophisticated enough mechanism of ethical checks and balances to withstand the onslaught of maneuvering from the wealthy who have more than enough means to affect such. The scale of these sophistications pale in comparison to what modern statecraft achieves though policing and monitoring today. States around the globe manage to monitor movements of suspected criminals (who know they're being monitored), or collect taxes through efficient means, for example. There are no reasons why similar measures couldn't be taken to ensure that ptoxocracy is safeguarded within reason, especially if a given state holds ptoxocracy as a good within society. One such mechanism would be the outright elimination of political donors in campaign finance.

Ptoxocracy is thoroughly pragmatic. The achievements of powerful governments like the United States are generally the outcomes of the desires of those eligible officeholders with power to sway and determine government policy. Any government that desires checks and balances on power will likely accomplish those aims. Although we lack meaningful ethical restraints on officials in our present historical circumstance, as the case of the COVID-related briefings mentioned in the first chapter demonstrates,

---

5. Biden, "Full Transcript," para. 12.
6. Biden, "Full Transcript," para. 12.

we do so not because ethical constraints are impossible, but because the ruling class desires freedom from checks and balances. The fact of corruption, however, does not make accountability impossible. It is because the ruling class is overwhelmingly composed of the rich that policies holding rich rulers accountable are so difficult to achieve.

Ptoxocracy in practice is relatively straightforward. Let's imagine that it is time to elect a new slate of city council members for a midsize municipality. All the existing measures for seeking one's name on the ballot are in place, including proof of residency and age and the collection of nomination signatures from a specific number of local residents (all eligibility requirements). The only thing that needs to change is the addition of one simple verification that demonstrates proof of one's income and financial holdings as below a certain threshold. This could be the federal poverty line, or a particular number determined by each municipality, but a verifying body (likely the same as verify age and residence) would examine one's income via tax statements, bank accounts, and the like, to determine eligibility. Once demonstrated that they fulfill all the eligibility requirements, a potential candidate could have their name moved forward into election cycles for consideration by voters.

We can just as easily imagine a similar situation for other officeholders. Let us imagine a state not unlike the United States around the turn of the twenty-first century, with all its existing policies, laws, military capacities, global relationships, and flourishing artistic, religious, nonprofit, business, and civil society. Now, imagine that come election season, the only eligible persons for office are the materially poor, depending on the eligibility requirement which a society implements in a ptoxocratic manner. For this example, let's keep it simple and say that this society has concocted some form of eligibility requirement for potential candidates in which no one with title of property, including but not limited to their names on an estate for inheritance, is eligible for elected office throughout the nation at any level of government. This means that all judges, state officials, governors, treasurers, city council members, county sheriffs, federal legislators, and even the executive are of a sort of class that exists apart from those we might call the rich. In this case, not one of the thousands of elected officials are landowners. (It should be noted that land ownership may not be the best eligibility requirement, but it is a simple marker of wealth and serves to help our imaginations flourish.)

In such a society, persons holding power within legislative, judicial, and executive branches—that is, policymaking, enforcement, and justice-making—all have some form of stake in the lives of the poor because they themselves are poor. Poverty is structural in nature and requires a structural solution. In general, one is not individually poor apart from family, friends, and social circles. Outside of the limited circumstances of asceticism in which wealth is intentionally rejected as a way of life because of one's religious or moral belief systems, it is rare for people of the lower economic classes to move in social circles of the higher classes. American society functions on class segregation, not only in obvious places where entry into high society is purchased or denoted, but in the schools, neighborhoods, churches, and homes we choose to inhabit. It is likely that those from among the poor immediately have a stake in the lives of the poor because their closest friends, family, and communities are also poor. They, at a bare minimum, understand something of poverty merely by their proximity to it, and their familiarity (at a basic level) with being people who do not own land. Such people may identify with one another, if not on a cultural or geographic location, with the very basic experience of dealing with rents, landlords, and rental insurance. When elected to office, if they wish to continue holding that office, persons must maintain their status as non-land-owning for the duration of their official term.

Imagine what this government might accomplish on behalf of the growing number of persons who are renters. It's not hard to see that their priorities would emerge out of direct experience with slum lords, inequitable treatment of non-land-owning persons, and so on. It is not hard to imagine a ptoxocratic judge being more capable of setting aside the biases that often emerge when social class and status distance land-owning judiciaries from persons who rent. This government's authority rests in elected persons who have not a stake in the well-being or continued enrichment of the wealthy, but a stake in the well-being of the poor. This is not to say that landowners would be banned or discouraged from continuing to purchase and own even more land, but that they would be ineligible to belong to the ruling class which tends to govern toward its own betterment. In this case their possession of land renders them ineligible. Again, in order to imagine such a government, we must jettison our personal biases against the poor as undereducated, unhygienic, improper, and the like. These biases exist as a wall to the imagination and are ultimately unhelpful.

It is not difficult to see the ways in which those with a stake in the lives of renters might govern in completely different ways than landholders. Now, this example sets eligibility requirements at a conservative level, for it is certainly possible for one to have loads of cash and yet still not own land. Let's imagine that the eligibility bar for potential elected officials is set more aggressively, say, at the poverty line. Since it was easy to imagine the ways that a class of rulers emerging from renters would prioritize the problems of renters when in power, it is not difficult to imagine the ways in which government by the financially poor might give rise to a trove of other policy and political decisions. We know the connections between ecological devastation, pollution, and poverty through empirical study like *Toxic Wastes and Race* (1987), a first-of-its-kind study sponsored by the Commission for Racial Justice of the United Church of Christ that demonstrated exactly these links. We can imagine that during times of economic calamity, for example, such policy makers would likely first examine the cost of stock market crashes and troubles upon the most vulnerable rather than upon those who can most afford it, and while taking the positive effects of the banking system into consideration, might include policy solutions for both the poor and the banking sectors. What would it mean to have a legislative branch whose primary interest was the de-exploitation of the poor? Today, a disproportionate percentage of greenhouse gas is emitted by the rich, but the effect is disproportionately felt by the poor. The poor are more in tune with the implications of noxious gas emissions, as these tend to be an afterthought of current policy. One can imagine a ptoxocratic society in which the dangers of ecological devastation would not be borne solely by the poor but might be more equitably shared by all classes, thereby leading to a downward trend in ecological devastation.

The effects of an eligibility requirement would further the aims of racial equity as well in such a country. Beyond ecological policy, what would the policies of poor lawmakers say about military spending (and recruitment techniques), entitlement spending, and immigration reform? How might these giants of public policy be shaped by those who have an interest in the well-being of the poor? Little has changed, for example, for persons of color in the United States when it comes to homeownership versus renting. Black Americans still own a far smaller share of homes than do their white counterparts. White Americans are disproportionately wealthier than Black Americans, so that as long as wealth is an entry point to political power, policies will always fail to address the underlying causes of inequality. If, still using our imaginations, the only eligible candidates for office were non-property-holding persons over the age of 18 in any given jurisdiction or election boundary, then it follows that a higher proportion of Black and disenfranchised persons would be eligible to stand for election than whites, which means that for the first time in American history, the nation might begin to have a ruling class that reflects the diversity of human life within its borders.

Most importantly, within this imagined (and much-changed) society, the rich would have a true stake in the lives of the poor. If the poor are the only eligible candidates for office, and the rich truly seek to look out for their fortunes, it follows that the rich would encourage the most talented from within the eligible pool of poor persons to run for elected office. Suddenly education and mentorship of the poor becomes a worthwhile task whose benefit is felt across all sectors, communities, and classes. Suddenly the nation's most prestigious sites for higher education would begin competing for the poor, hoping to win poor students into their ranks to win future ruling class citizens. Colleges and universities already pander to classes of persons who eventually might become powerful, so imagining their pivot to a new base of future power brokers is not much of a leap.

With investment from organizations and systems, as well as wealthy individuals, comes a new problem, however. These highly educated poor now have a choice: do the newly educated and world-class students enter public life as they have been groomed, or do they seek to use their education to enhance their material well-being? Here we see the horrific inequality baked into such a system without an eligibility requirement. A system of government without a restriction allows elected individuals to have it both ways, and usually this means that officeholders bounce seamlessly between private industry and elected position or bureaucratic appointment, enriching themselves and their industry partners with favorable policies along the way. Ptoxocracy avoids this trap entirely by giving the poor a true path: either you may become poor, or you may freely pursue wealth. Choosing the latter security is no harm to society, and possibly even a good, and perhaps is the better path for one's family and ultimate well-being. This latter path cuts one off from political power. In either case the goal of equality and opportunity has been met: this once-poor person has now found their way into a new life of potential material gain through a quality education. They have ended the cycle of generational powerlessness, if not poverty itself, for themselves or their family. They have surrendered access to one form of power and thereby gained access to another.

A government that seeks the highest good for the lowest among its own is ptoxocratic in nature because it now holds a meaningful stake in the lives of the poor and will be a government that lifts all members of society together. This is the true aim of ptoxocratic government: that policymakers hold a noncoerced stake in the outcome of the lives of the poor, whose effect is the betterment of all society.

Ensuring that elected leaders maintain poverty while holding power is key to the ptoxocratic system. Poverty and power are like oil and water, as opposite to one another as can be imagined, and maintaining this separation would be difficult. Wealth and ruling power hold a magnetic connection to one another: political power grants access to wealth, and wealth grants access to ruling power. This was as true in the Roman Republic as it is in Soviet Russia. Occasionally the poor (or middle-class) ruler will emerge onto the political scene, elected democratically or through revolutionary means. It is rare, however, for that one to stay poor. Political power will bring connections and opportunities that this person could never have had before, as the wealthy seek to influence the statesman by means of their own wealth. The poor tyrant, likewise, gains access to the tools of his own wealth creation by way of the government's monopoly of state violence. Lenin may have been the working class's hero, penniless in Switzerland as revolution brewed at home, but he did not die a penniless worker's death.

Speaking of Marxist ideology, it is time to quash an implicit criticism of ptoxocracy before it is uttered. Ptoxocracy is not Marxist ideology dressed up in a new form. There is a fashionable line of criticism by some that sees the mere identification of class distinction within systems of power as the appropriation of Marxist ideology. The ancient Romans, by this logic, were Marxist insofar as they established eligibility requirements for officeholders based on wealth and land-owning status. There is nothing inherently Marxist about identifying economic status as a marker of power; in fact this is what the rich have been doing by way of the mythology of the rich ruling class throughout history. Affirming that wealth status should indeed be considered when determining leadership status, ptoxocracy seizes initiative in the opposite direction. Ptoxocracy agrees with the historical claim that one's economic status establishes a precondition for ruling authority, yet it argues that those who possess the most wealth generally make the worst rulers. To argue otherwise is to employ the mythology of the rich ruling class, to claim that wealth entitles one to power, or makes for a good political ruler.

So far we have seen how ptoxocracy could yield candidates whose interests serve a far greater range of citizens, a deeper and more thoughtful set of actions on important issues, and might help break cycles of poverty for all. It could also serve up a more peaceful set of candidates. I do not mean to imply that the wealthy are naturally vicious or violent. But history demonstrates the ways that business interests and national interests collide far too easily on a global scale, and nations send their sons and daughters to war at the whims of the rich whose aims are not in the interest of the people at large. Furthermore, the ranks of today's enlisted soldiers are rarely filled with the rich, as military service acts as a means by which a person can attain better social and economic status. Armies directed by a commander in chief who comes from among the poor will more truly appreciate the costs of war than will a rich man whose son has no need to better himself by enlisting in the military. The poor, in this way, will have a better sense of the true cost of lives lost to communities and neighborhoods than their wealthy counterparts.

GREED

Before proceeding any further, we must explicitly deal with the most pressing and immediate concern that we have only so far touched upon without naming outright; that is, the reality of human greed. Ptoxocracy acknowledges wealth—and its most extreme expression, greed—as a persistent human aim, something that not only can drive informational expansion and technological capacity but can also create opportunities for society at large. We don't have to deny the benefits of material wealth to be opposed to its overreaching consequences. Perhaps the drive for material wealth is as close to a fundamental truth of human instinct as we can possibly imagine. Humans desire material goods: homes, food, vacations, entertainments, information technologies, and so on. Ptoxocracy allows for a variance in human demand of goods: the ascetic and ultrarich may live side by side under this system, even as the rich are unable to attain political governmental power. Likewise, even those who agree with wealth's moral abhorrence can live peacefully in ptoxocracy among the rich, as they are given a share in political power previously unavailable to them. Ptoxocracy understands that the true danger in wealth, as it pertains to the poor, as it regards the noninterest of the rich toward the poor, is its currency as the basis of exchange for power, especially political power.

No amount of religion, education, moral argumentation, societal good, policy, or otherwise, has ever or will ever rid human beings of the capacity and tendency for greed. Further, a great temptation to ptoxocracy as a concept is the idealization of the *ptoxoi*—that is, the assumption that the poor are intrinsically morally better people than the rich. Oliver Twist may elicit pathos, but we must not make the mistake of allowing such idealizations to form into concrete ideas and policies. We must, in fact, stamp out this assumption immediately and outrightly: any argument for ptoxocracy cannot and will not succeed so long as it rests upon the inherent ethical goodness of the *ptoxoi*. In fact, we must account for the idea that the poor are no more or no less ethical people than the rich, and that they are as prone to the temptations and whims of greed as any other class of persons. The poor are simply the rich without money—that is, there is no ethical or moral difference in predisposition between them. Any argument that begins otherwise is doomed to failure. There are ethically good rich and morally corrupt poor, just as there are morally corrupt rich and ethically good poor. Ptoxocracy does not rest on the assertion of a moral or ethical goodness of the *ptoxoi*. Rather, the argument necessarily recognizes the reality of human greed as a given that immediately needs a response. While I have previously argued against some forms of givenness, this is a given that we must adopt before proceeding: all human behavior is susceptible, consciously or unconsciously, to greed. Ptoxocracy must account for this to be a viable idea, and one we shall say more about later.

Until now, we have spoken very little of the middle classes. One might argue that the middle class has more to lose than the rich under ptoxocratic system. On the one hand, they are now cut off from upward mobility via political action, having exceeded the eligibility requirements of ptoxocracy. Perhaps a middle-class person would feel frustrated that their well-earned savings accounts and prudent financial planning early in life should cut them from political power. Rightly so. While there are not so many in power today in the American government who might truly pass the eligibility tests of a ptoxocratic system as we have imagined it, there are many more who are strongly middle class in their net worth and investment holdings. If a healthy democracy is one in which the middle class can thrive, why not opt for a system of government in which the middle class rule?

The middle class only has the most to lose in ptoxocracy if their belief in meritocracy and the mythology of the ruling class is ironclad. By contrast, however, ptoxocracy continues to be the most truly equitable modification to governance, even for this group. The argument for middle-class solidarity with ptoxocracy is simple, though it first requires one to jettison their belief in today's meritocracy and its underpinning mythology of the ruling class. As it happens now as under a system without economic eligibility requirements, the rich tend to horde both wealth and political power. Again, since wealth and political authority are two forms of power, these tend to rise to the top and then stay in the top. Interests become entrenched, and the rich begin asking how they can make themselves even richer, as observed in congressional responses early in the pandemic. One of the ways they can do so is via political power, or at least through the manipulation of political power. As such, middle-class interests are secondary to the interests of the rich and teased as valuable only when one rich ruler needs to score political points against the other, either within one's own party or against another party.

Ptoxocracy cuts off the rich from power, thereby opening a channel for governmental participation to the poor and ultimately recreating meritocracy for both the poor and the middle class. Again, a person may be politically powerful or rich, but not both. This also means, as is common today, that most people simply stay out of politics and enjoy their middle-class lives, ambivalent to power, neither rising into public esteem nor striking it rich. By severing the connection between wealth and power, a ptoxocratic society opens a new pathway into a form of power for the middle class, if only for those who would choose it. A middle-class person can willingly give up a certain amount of their wealth to become eligible for elected office. Certain religious persons do this already when taking on vows to serve a particular order or sect, so that it is not completely unimaginable that a middle-class person might sacrifice personal wealth for the sake of something perceived to be of greater value. If a truly able person wishes to become powerful, all they need to do is give up their claim to wealth until they fall beneath the eligibility standard. That is far easier a task for worthy potential candidates than becoming wealthy, which entails further entrenching one's stake in the interests of the wealthy. Likewise, the middle-class person who truly believes that being rich would fill their innermost desires can work as hard as they want to gain wealth. Nothing changes on that front except that they, like the rich, may not use the mechanisms of political office to enrich themselves.

Middle-class persons, then, have a new way into political power that involves freedom of choice, voluntary action, and election by one's community. In our present historical political landscape, a wishful candidate needs vast sums of money to be elected to office, money which is either borrowed, won by campaign promises to wealthy donors, or out of one's pocket. Without funds of some kind one's chances are slim at winning office. Ptoxocracy eliminates the need for the rich to be involved in financing or underwriting candidates, rendering the middle class free from the gatekeeping tendencies of the wealthy.

CONCLUSION

Under ptoxocracy, reaching the eligibility for office is a free choice for anyone to make simply by the act of making themselves poor. This, of course, is not a guarantor of election, but the possibility of election between poor, middle class, and rich is now truly equal. By injecting a simple eligibility criterion for election, the field becomes truly equal in regard to political power. No one can buy their way into office, since a condition for holding office is the absence of wealth. Wealth, in other words, becomes an unchangeable currency toward political power. Moreover, by injecting such an eligibility requirement into representative democratic processes, all of society, most especially the rich, are given a meaningful stake in the lives of the poor, which previously only occurs when the rich opt into such a stake by way of moral obligation and charity. Because moral obligation and charity are optional, they are feeble, and rendered useless at the whims of the rich. Ptoxocracy institutes a permanent bridge, the kind of which might bridge a chasmic divide of the sort Jesus's story of Lazarus illumines.

4

Interrogating Ptoxocracy

ONE OF THE BEST WAYS to explore possible futures is to let that new idea wander through the world of existing realities. Once we have worked to understand our biases, curiously and lovingly rooting these out to let the newness of an idea come into full appreciation, we can explore an idea with a sense of adventure rather than dread. Ptoxocracy is a new idea that I imagine brings a sense of anxiety to those, like me, who are rich. Edwin Friedman, examining the ways that such anxiety can stifle new and beautiful possible futures, writes, "There is a relationship between risk and reality that involves not risk and one's *sense of reality*, which is a psychological concept, but nerve and *reality itself*. For if imagination involves risk, the willingness to risk is critical to validating one's perceptions."[1] Ptoxocracy as a modification or enhancement to representational democracy requires deeper investigation because it entails risk for every citizen. The reward for such risk is a monumental shift within the structures of society that give rise to greater care of the poor, which in turn, yields a stronger society. This chapter takes the implications of ptoxocracy seriously enough to interrogate the effect of ptoxocracy on issues of import, ranging from national security and international politics to judiciary appointments and compensation of elected officials, as well as examining the extent to which society might be improved (or not) by ptoxocratic leadership. What follows are serious interrogations taken in the spirit of curiosity rather than anxiety. If we care about the poor enough to reimagine the foundational structures of the relationship between ruling authority and wealth, we ought to take a

1. Friedman, *Failure of Nerve*, 43.

moment to interrogate some of the implications that could arise from such possible futures.

The aim of such an interrogation is to free ptoxocracy from the unfortunate tendency whereby today's well-meaning ideas become tomorrow's oppressive ideologies. Oppressive ideologies, as a rule, tend to resist interrogation. Hannah Arendt, examining the legacy of seemingly good-faith ideas that form the basis of destructive totalitarian movements in history, writes, "Ideologies always assume that one idea is sufficient to explain every thing in the development from the premise, and that no experience can teach anything because everything is comprehended in this consistent process of logical deduction."[2] To interrogate ptoxocracy is to free it from the authoritarian temptation toward its own myopia, which is to understand it as a modification to existing democratic structures without falling prey to the ideological risks in Arendt's warning. To imagine ptoxocracy as beneficial to society, we must allow it to crash against the complexities of our everyday lives, as well as the structures already in place, and to examine the wreckage through the lens of justice, equality, and the social well-being of those whom it aims to empower.

Pastorally, I encounter exactly these kinds of seemingly painful interrogations all the time, yet the fruit they produce most often enhances rather than detracts. I take refuge in the words of Cynthia Lindner, who encourages congregational pastors that "being faithful, by definition, requires participating in change rather than resisting it."[3] This chapter, then, offers a participatory attempt at beginning to interrogate the many implications of ptoxocracy, though it is only a starting point. The hope is to give the reader a sense of methodology in this interrogative process. Taking ptoxocracy seriously means that questions and criticisms will arise, and the hope of this chapter is to encourage readers to raise those concerns for themselves. Such an interrogation rewards the risk of the imagination.

Within ptoxocracy, the poor now have practical access to true decision-making functions in governmental authority, and the policies that flow from leadership by the poor would benefit a greater number of persons. It is not surprising that everything from military spending to zoning laws, licensing for new drilling in the Arctic, and migrant policies would be deeply affected by a body of lawmakers who have a true stake in the lives of the poor. Again, this does not mean that they would not have a stake in

---

2. Arendt, *Origins of Totalitarianism*, 617.
3. Lindner, *Varieties of Gifts*, 66.

the lives of the rich and middle classes. It also does not mean that they are not prone to corruption, greed, or even faulty decision-making. Moreover, it does not even entail that their policies are the best of all possible policies. It is, however, to say that they would have a perspective as rulers that the rich do not insofar as they are more likely to have a true stake in the lives of the poor. This is the fundamental alteration of the status quo as we know it, the single most important innovation that ptoxocracy begets to society: the poor are not forgotten.

Whether one harbors unconscious or conscious biases against the poor, it is perfectly fair to poke and prod a political innovation like ptoxocracy. There are, of course, endless questions to ask of any political system, and at the end of the day trial and error may be the final arbiter of an idea. The intention here is to ask meaningful questions of the idea rather than to set up straw arguments to push over without much of a fuss.

INTERROGATING PTOXOCRACY: COMPLICATIONS, PROBLEMS, AND CRITICISMS

Challenging the Frame

We begin the interrogation with an immediate challenge to the underlying premise the gives rise to the ptoxocratic assertions. In chapter 2, we framed the argument for ptoxocracy within the problem of both the injustice of the mythology of the rich ruling class as well as the incapacity of the rich to hold a meaningful stake in the lives of the poor. One immediate counterargument to ptoxocracy, then, might to be to argue that rulers need not hold a stake in the lives of every citizen to be capable of ruling them well, legislating on their behalf, overseeing mechanisms of judicial power, and executing laws. A judge need not hold a stake in the well-being of every person she sees to render justice; in fact, holding a stake in the personal well-being of persons within her courtroom might be the very fact upon which she must recuse herself. In other words, holding a stake in the well-being of a person might lead to making worse decisions than better ones, or at least raise a host of conflicts of interest. This is indeed a substantial challenge to the foundations of ptoxocracy, for in failing to identify the rich wielding power problematically if they do not hold a stake in the lives of the poor, we lose the thrust of the project entirely.

A parallel way of arguing this point is to say that the rich do not necessarily hold a stake in the lives of the rich, and that they seem to function well enough without one as rulers in regard to the rich. In other words, the CEOs of Exxon Mobile and Microsoft, two of the most highly rated corporations in the world, do not need to hold a stake in the well-being of one another's existence in order to function within an economic system that continues to allow their businesses to flourish. In fact, they might very well argue that a system that held a stake in their well-being might be a hindrance to their flourishing, and that more attention from the other company might frustrate that flourishing. In other words, holding a stake in the well-being of citizens matters very little, if not at all, in the flourishing of persons who are, in fact, themselves already flourishing. So why might we claim it is of such importance for the poor?

My response to this counterargument comes by way of analogy, one which I am admittedly less knowledgeable of than a host of others, though I will try my best to entertain the contours of the analogy for both the expert and novice alike. It is an argument from international soccer leagues. This is not an analogy about the way the game is played; rather, it is one of the structures that support the game itself.

The top professional league for soccer in the United States is called Major League Soccer (MLS). The MLS is comprised of thirty teams, all of whom compete against one another in league play throughout the year. Some of these teams, say the Seattle Sounders and Portland Timbers, host bitter rivalries as in any other sport. They are, for all intents and purposes, as close to enemies within the league as possible. At the very least they are ambivalent about one another's success, much like Microsoft and Exxon Mobile, yet in this case they are adversaries, so that when one of the teams does poorly, the other celebrates, and vice versa. Their individual flourishing, in fact, comes at the direct expense of the other. Since only one of these can ultimately be the league champion, one must always lose out to the other.

As intense or ambivalent as the rivalry is at a given moment, the consequences of either team losing or winning are different from other soccer leagues. The English Premier League, like it's American counterpart, is the top league for soccer players in Great Britain. Unlike its US counterpart, however, the Premier League does not exist within the same sort of framework as the MLS. Instead, it acts in concert with no less than seven other tiers of leagues, a pyramid of skill within which it sits at the top. The effect of being the worst teams in this league system is relegation. Relegation entails that the bottom three teams of the Premier League go into the lower-tier league (oddly named the Championship League), and the top three teams in this latter league move upward into the Premier League. So, bitter rivals of English soccer, say Manchester United and Liverpool, also exist, and the stakes are much higher for both teams due to the possible consequences of a season loss—namely, relegation, which yields an exit from the tier of a league altogether. As fans of the Premier League know, relegation is a meaningful threat.

The point here is that the mere existence of another system of league formation—that is, that a league could conceive of itself differently than the MLS—points to something true of the MLS that the seeming rivalry between Portland and Seattle would otherwise mask: namely, that the two US clubs would seem to hold more of a stake in the well-being of one another than, say, Liverpool and Manchester. Rivalries are good for business, and just as it can be true that two companies competing against one another can lead to flourishing by way of zealous creativity and the like, so too do the Sounders and Timbers help one another flourish, though they are seemingly rivals. The point here is that their respective club governing boards and CEOs don't need to hold a stake in the company of the other for the mere existence of a rival to be of benefit to them. In other words, it seems that the MLS functions as a universe unto its own, giving rise to a system that appears to hold bitter enmity and rivalry, yet this is but a stage upon which the whole league enacts a relatively inconsequential drama. No one is punished for coming in last place in the MLS because there is no relegation. The structure matters. The same is true of rich persons. They may appear as bitter enemies to one another, not holding a stake in one another's lives, but the mere presence of the one is the very thing that bolsters and supports and validates the other. They need not hold a stake or care for the well-being of the other—and may very well say and act in contrary ways—but they exist within a system constituted on the behalf of wealthy persons within which they are given the opportunity to flourish. They're in the same league, even if bitter rivals. A more equitable system would allow for other entities to enter the league (by analogy, this is the English football league system) by way of true meritocracy.

My point here is that indeed the rich (like the Sounders and Timbers) may appear as enemies but are, in fact, de facto stakeholders of one another by virtue of holding a common interest in the structure that allows them each to find ways to translate the powers of wealth into the powers of politics, and vice versa. The current system of government is indeed much like the MLS—major players seem at odds with one another yet are still part of the league if they lose, and therefore actually do hold a stake in one another's well-being. While they don't hold a stake in one another's well-being (per se), they do hold stock in the MLS, which in turn, holds stock in all of them. Ptoxocracy, by contrast, is a modification to democracy that yields a democratic system that looks (by analogy) much more like the English football league system—that is, an equitable system within which teams may enter top-tier league play from all levels, even from the very bottom. It is not a system that substitutes a league comprised of the rich for a league comprised of the poor. Rather, it is a system that offers on-ramps into the game for those at all levels of participation. Meritocracy appears to function in this way for the poor in regard to ruling power, but as we have seen, fails because the unspoken rules of the structures (namely, the mythology of the rich ruling class) keep certain, if not most, persons from gaining actual entry to political power.

The Self-Enriching Ptoxocrat (Part One)

We must return to deal with the historical conundrum of human greed that arises almost immediately as an implication of any political apparatus, this time to examine the impact of greed on the ptoxocrat. In the previous chapter we examined the tendency of greed to inform the transfer of wealth into political power, so that it is only fair that we examine this same dynamic in ptoxocracy from the opposite direction. What if the person elected to office within a ptoxocratic system should use their newfound governmental authority as a means of self-enrichment? History bears this out repeatedly in every system of human governance, and ptoxocracy is not immune to it. This is both a problem for ptoxocracy and a good place to begin identifying implications of this structure. One might see it as an inevitable conclusion that impoverished persons now occupying a seat at the table of authority would seek to use their newfound authority as a mechanism for self-improvement and personal gain. The problem rests on a universal assumption of human greed, and of the magnetic qualities of wealth and power.

I take it to be a fundamental truth that power and wealth are coexistent, and that one may beget the other if not for a necessary guardrail inhibiting the inevitable. Again, however, societies place limits, checks, eligibility requirements, and balances on all sorts of behaviors of their ruling class, checks and balances that anticipate exactly this sort of human behavior already. The mythology of the rich ruler is the only thing stopping us from placing a similar limit to this natural coupling. Is a person's economic status so uniquely special that it should not receive some kind of check or balance against using one's personal wealth to further enrich themselves by way of governing authority? Is wealth more unique than age as an eligibility requirement? Is wealth more unique to the person than national citizenship? By no means. Wealth is so deviously magnetic to political power that it should, perhaps, receive the most vigorous treatment. US elected leadership has, time and time again, demonstrated the ways in which a system that relies on self-policing and ethics by custom rather than policy has been deeply troubling. Ptoxocracy absolutely needs policy and ethical guardrails to keep power and wealth from infecting one another, as much as nonptoxocratic systems do.

The rich use political power for their personal enrichment. This is as true of the US Congress as it was for Napoleon Bonaparte. The question is whether the poor hold some special disposition so as to avoid the magnetic attraction and implication of one to the other. Absolutely not: the poor are no less or no more inclined to use positions of authority, or the exposure and opportunities that such positions bring, to enrich themselves. Former US officials today amass large sums of money through speaking fees and book deals. Do we expect that the poor might be immune from such means of personal gain? Do we expect that publishers would cease offering retrospective policy memoir contracts to poor and former office holders? By no means. These and many other opportunities for self-betterment will necessarily present themselves as opportunities. The novelty of ptoxocracy versus, say, Marxism, is that ptoxocracy lends no moral judgment against that poor person who should use former political authority as a means of enrichment. In fact, ptoxocracy is totally ambivalent to the point of saying that perhaps society is all the better for it, having accomplished a system in which a once-poor person gained access to power and therefore self-betterment.

Self-enrichment may, in fact, be a natural outcome of power, and the question is to what degree ptoxocracy can regulate self-enrichment while a governmental official holds power. We remember that governmental and elected officials are already subject to ethical inquiries (though some of these laws are better prosecuted or investigated than others). There's no reason to believe that a ptoxocratic system might require more or fewer policies on the dangers of governmental authority translated into personal gain. Make no mistake, the poor ruler will be tempted and taunted by the wealthy to influence policy matters, to recouple the unity of wealth and power at every turn. Today we see the ways that public servants and private industry leaders leapfrog to and from public to private life, enriching themselves and the corporate interests they serve along the way. It is a strange set of bureaucratic norms when former energy executives hold positions of governmental oversight and decision-making over the very industries within which they cut their teeth. Those relationships unfortunately do not disappear under ptoxocracy, and this is one dynamic the system may be incapable of changing so long as that system maintains its capitalistic economic leanings. It is not hard to imagine a poor civil servant tempted by the interests of the wealthy in the same way and tilting the hand of government policy in the direction of one or another company in exchange for personal gain. Ptoxocracy cannot stop this.

Ptoxocracy can, however, persist in eligibility requirements regardless of a former politician's choices for self-enrichment. First and foremost, ptoxocracy must take existing ethical policies into serious effect, that much is simple when it comes to stemming the human tendency of corruption and greed. Easy enough. Second, to avoid losing a stake in the eligibility for government office, ptoxocracy must be not only limited to the moment that a person decides to seek office, but throughout their time in office. To hold office, one must continue to live beneath the threshold of eligibility. Whether the eligibility requirement has to do with one's net worth or one's land-ownership status, this requirement must be met throughout their time in office. Again, there is nothing particularly novel about the idea of perpetual eligibility. I am, as a pastor, asked to attend constantly to my skill sets and professional enrichment by way of continuing education and taking care of myself. If I fall devastatingly ill, then it is the duty of my board to find a replacement, someone whose fitness for the job renders them able to complete pastoral tasks that my illness might not. The same should be true of governmental authorities. The idea of eligibility in perpetuity is not a novel one.

The Self-Enriching Ptoxocrat (Part Two)

Let's imagine a situation, however, in which a perfectly able elected official who has kept their eligibility requirement intact is now facing the end of their governmental term in office and is given the opportunity to work in the private sector. Should that person decline the offer out of some moral or ethical basis? Would they be breaking faith with the tenets of ptoxocracy by enriching themselves with new opportunities as they turn from public service toward private? This is the easiest of all questions to answer. Of course this former office-holder should accept a new private industry position! Of course their time in government should serve as a means for self-enrichment, so long as those means are ethical and legal. Get a lucrative book deal! Sign a contract with a streaming television company to tell your story in government as a ruler! By all means, enrich yourself! The rich do this all the time to no one's benefit but their own. However, the individual in question must return to that basic tenet of ptoxocratic systems: one may be rich, or one may be politically powerful, but one may never be both at once. Once they have elevated themselves and their family into a new economic reality, this person is no longer eligible for office, as they no longer hold an actual stake in the lives of the poor. Perhaps they harbor good feelings or interests that go beyond those of their rich contemporaries. Fine. But they are no longer eligible for ruling power. Fitness for office is not based in moral capacity or one's compassion, it is based in economic reality. It is as simple as that. Perhaps they are extremely generous and well-natured to the poor, remembering their own experience of poverty. Does this give them eligibility for governance once again? No. In this way ptoxocracy is unsentimental. The fact of their eligibility rests entirely on their present economic status.

Let's now imagine that a member of Congress serving a six-year term decides to enrich themself legally by way of book deals or other legal and ethical means halfway through their term. This, too, is simple: they must vacate the position immediately so that a new candidate can assume authority by way of the usual channels of election. We already have mechanisms for such conditions.

In this way we can see a secondary effect of ptoxocracy as a means through which the poor can better themselves. In this way, suddenly the rich do have a stake in the lives of the poor. Not only might the rich begin supporting the educations and well-being of poor persons—for these poor may one day be their rulers—but the poor take on a new value as persons with vital experience and knowledge. They might become lobbyists or specialists in dealing with governmental systems. Society might be so much the better for it, in fact, to gain a wide perspective such as this. Today these positions are held by wealthy persons whose perspective is limited regarding the poor. Ptoxocracy serves, then, as something of an equalizer. By giving the poor access to power, and cutting the wealthy off from that same access, we open a new means by which the poor can lift beyond the wretchedness of poverty. Of course, there will be those who actively choose poverty because of the allure of political power. And so much the better! Imagine a landscape of deft policymakers who actively decide against self-enrichment because they desire to stay in power. History bears out examples of such persons, as in the case of the late John Lewis, who did exactly this. Imagine the future of the United States if the structure of political authority gave rise to the potential of multiple leaders like John Lewis, the way that such persons could absolutely benefit our society through creative solutions to complex challenges. One imagines that they would be far more likely to work side by side with political opponents, for example, since self-enrichment is not their explicit aim.

If the poor are the only eligible candidates for elected positions, then it follows that the rich would have a stake in educating them for excellence in leadership. Today one must either be exceptionally talented to be accepted into a world-class hall of higher education, a legacy admission, or wealthy. We would expect to see that, at a minimum, it would be in the best interest of not only the schools in question but society at large that world-class colleges offer a greater portion of scholarships and admittances to the poor, as the poor will soon be governing. In fact, we might begin to see a true meritocracy emerge, rather than the fictitious mythology of meritocracy that we see today in higher education.

This is to say little upon examination thus far of the effect upon policy-making decisions themselves. The poor are not better suited for statecraft than the rich. In fact, speaking strictly along the lines of education and capacity (at least in the infancy of ptoxocracy), the poor may not be as skillful as previous rich rulers had been in crafting policy. While I don't believe that the rich are inherently skillful at creating equitable policy today, one must admit that an Ivy League education, purchased or earned, has its benefits. These institutions are world-class for a reason, despite their truly inequitable admissions policies. Yet one can imagine that the scope of policy-making decisions by a ptoxocratic set of rulers will address a wider range of interests than today's policymakers have time to address. Numerous studies over the past ten years have illuminated the amount of time each member of Congress is expected to spend in fundraising if they hope to be reelected, revealing that as much as half of their time is spent this way. Imagine what policymakers could accomplish if they were free from the demands of fundraising among the rich. Either through what are called *partial public-funding* election approaches or *full public-funding* election approaches, the United States could dramatically change the outsized power the rich have in determining election cycles. Both approaches seek a realignment of money and politics by way of public funding of political campaigns, taking disproportionate size of wealthy interests as an unhelpful given.[4]

National Security and Ptoxocracy

Matters of national security would be profoundly shifted under a ptoxocratic government. Just as a ptoxocratic system could open a means for self-enrichment for the poor, the military has been a means through which impoverished persons better themselves. A standing military, in other words, provides great opportunity for poor persons to climb a ladder of meritocracy and earn their way out of poverty. Elected officials today pay lip-service to the value of human life as they make grave decisions when sending troops into battle. Yet the examples of today's political leaders in their own military service seems to be more like Octavian than that of Julius Caesar. Octavian, it is said, would grow sick or weak the night before battle, and never proved himself a soldiering emperor. Similarly, one president of the United States famously avoided entrance into the draft during the Vietnam conflict due to alleged bone spurs, a curious anomaly of military expulsion brought to light by a family doctor. This person also happens to be one of the nation's wealthiest presidents to ever sit in office. A military whose commander in chief is a poor person would likely take decisions on when to go to war and with what troops much more seriously than a rich person.

Yet the argument goes even deeper when it comes to national security. How many wars in the history of the world have been fought by the many at the behest of the few and their interests? It is a curious thing when

4. Fouirnaies, "Public Funding of US Elections."

the former governor of Texas, the oil capital of the US, should become president of the United States, only to lock the nation in a multi-year, multi-trillion-dollar war with one of the world's leading oil-producing nations. It is even more curious when this former governor has financial interests in the well-being of the energy sector, and that much of his own personal wealth is tied to their fortunes. It is easy to see how the poor might not, in other words, drag a nation into war so easily for personal enrichment, as the poor would be free from the fiduciary duties accompanying those who hold a stake in the profitability of petroleum products. When the military is run by a poor commander in chief, suddenly that person has a stake in the well-being of the people serving under them, and these latter are not simply pawns in the global chessboard of personal enrichment. Moreover, and more to the point for this argument, a poor commander in chief lacks a connection to personal gain to be won through military intervention. Ptoxocracy gives rise to a more peaceful society, then, because it gives rise to a government whose aims are less distorted by personal self-enrichment. Again, though the rich would be out of power, they are free to pursue their own self-enrichment, though they may not do so while masquerading as selfless civil servants. The capacity of a ptoxocratic democracy to be led into war through the whims of a poor president is much lower, though admittedly not completely diminished, than a rich president.

Ptoxocracy and the Judiciary

Until this point, we have spent much time talking about the policy-making decisions of the poor, and little in considering the benefit to a well-functioning judicial system in ptoxocracy. US judges, until very recently, have been considered the pinnacle of ethical behavior when it comes to the mixture of wealth and judgments of power. Yet contemporary examples of behavior among justices of the Supreme Court make one wonder whether a human being is ever truly free of the seemingly inevitable connection between wealth and power. One has to wonder whether exuberant trips on enormous yachts around the world do not make a difference in the adjudicatory prejudices of those in power and can only marvel at the preposterous notion that such gifts have no consequences on deliberation.

Admittedly, the most difficult branch of US government for ptoxocracy is the judicial branch, if only because of the lag between judicial appointments by elected executive and legislative officials. In other words, apart from jurisdictions in which judges are elected by the people, judges are appointed and confirmed in the most part, so that their ascent into power must take place following the ascent of democratically elected ptoxocratic leaders. It is not impossible that sitting judges might find ptoxocracy intolerable, and use the office of the court to, in fact, oppose ptoxocratic governance. It would not be the first time a judicial branch attempted to rewrite policy on behalf of the wealthy.

Yet a more significant challenge to ptoxocratic judges might be that legal education requires vast amounts of skill, time, and money. It is no coincidence that most seats of the Supreme Court are filled by graduates of just two Ivy League schools, nor that most elected or appointed judges have spent years practicing law in private or corporate settings. Graduate education at an elite school that gains one entry into the highest seats of power is not only expensive, but likely out of reach for most poor persons under current systems. Yet this is exactly the kind of inequality in relation to any form of self-betterment, be it access to education or public good or opportunity, that ptoxocracy seeks to correct. The fact that entry to the most elite forms of higher education serves as a barrier to entry to public office or judicial appointment would seem to further the argument for ptoxocracy, given the unequitable admissions practices of these institutions that privilege entry of the wealthy. We might, however, be invited to step back even further now and wonder about our given assumptions about how things in the world must take place. Are Yale or Harvard the only schools that prepare minds for deep thinking such as is required at the highest court in the land? These questions unsettle our assumptions and challenge us to think more creatively about the ways government can function overall, as well as the role of elite educations in public life in general. Again, however, the judiciary branches would need to fall under the eligibility requirement of ptoxocracy, and it is likely that some of the most ardent defense of wealth would come from this area of government, likely under the guise of loyalty to original intent or federalism.

It is also the case that the judiciary branch, the US Supreme Court excepted, already finds itself under the kinds of intense scrutiny of ethics that ptoxocracy demands. Judges are highly competent and self-conscious, apart from a relative few who abuse ethical loopholes and take advantage of their place in government. It is not out of the question to expect that most persons attracted to the judiciary under ptoxocracy are the kinds of persons who also understand the benefit of such a system.

INTERROGATING PTOXOCRACY

Enforcement of Ptoxocratic Values over Time

One of the early problems to emerge in ptoxocracy has to do with a mechanism of accountability and enforcement of ptoxocratic eligibility requirements. If, for example, a person must maintain a certain level of poverty to stay in office, it seems that a discussion of the practical curbs and measures to be taken to ensure compliance with these eligibility requirements must be in order. Admittedly, ptoxocracy would, in fact, require something of a bureaucratic office or system of accountability to function properly. Political norms that encourage self-reporting as a positive behavior of politicians, as we see the US system bulging dangerously beneath today, would be insufficient. Any criminal with an internet connection can figure out how to launder money through an untraceable source, and it is absolutely within the realm of possibilities that a politician might gain political office within a ptoxocracy by shielding their assets in untraceable offshore bank accounts, for example.

Yet even more complex is the question of familial wealth. Must the spouse of a politician seeking office also be poor? What of a fiancé or less formalized relationship like a serious romantic partner? The questions don't end there. What of familial wealth between generations? Might a rich person decide to give their possessions and wealth to their children or grandchildren to gain eligibility to govern? These questions are valid and must be dealt with early to proceed to any further conversation of ptoxocracy.

To the question of either spousal or generational wealth. If the ptoxocratic eligibility requirement depends on *individual* net worth or land possession, then it is plausible that a married couple might simply transfer all their assets into the possession of the other partner and gain access to power mutually by way of the poor spouse. In this case a set of codes like those employed by the IRS would be a helpful way to compartmentalize the reality of married people's owning more property than that allowed for a single person through a system of financial categories. That's the easy scenario. What is more difficult is the eligible child of a wealthy family. Of course, one possibility is including estate futures in one's net worth, as in, considering all ways in which one is wealthy by way of holding future interest in an estate through transfer at the time of death. This, however, merely kicks the can of accountability down the line. Any wealthy family has at its disposal entire teams of accountants and lawyers to move and shield assets from prying eyes. This is a tricky situation, indeed, as it begins to complicate the eligibility requirements of ptoxocracy, yielding an originally simple system that, in the end, becomes unwieldy.

Let's suppose the child of a wealthy family with large corporate holdings decides to run for office, and then further suppose that they have been urged to do so at the behest of their family to see that the interests of their business receive favorable policy treatment among lawmakers. They could easily give their assets back to their family (with an unwritten promise of future return) and become eligible, seemingly without consequence. It is conceivable that their family might help win the election via the vast wealth at their disposal while the candidate themselves might continue to fall well short of the eligibility requirement. The most basic solution is to rid our political landscape of external campaign finance altogether, and to strengthen authority to punish those who influence political elections via outside money. Similarly, perhaps candidates for office would be required to indicate whether they had given away large sums of money within the five years prior to seeking office. More extremely, a candidate might be required (rather than urged to do so by political norm) to disclose, say, five years of financial tax return documents when seeking election to office. In other words, there are clearly mechanisms to monitor and identify those who would seek to game the system.

There is another, more troubling situation that one can imagine quite easily, that of a poor citizen bribed by a wealthy one with promises of wealth following a term of office. While this conduct probably already falls outside of ethical boundaries of acceptable behavior, it's easy to imagine a way in which ptoxocracy could be completely undermined by a widespread practice of this mechanism of control. Through a network of promises and bribes the poor would become rulers in name only, thereby undermining the ptoxocracy entirely. To counter this threat, a policy would need to go into effect that both places the ultimate burden of consequence upon the wealthy and incentivizes the poor for identifying those who would threaten the common good through bribery. Loosely sketched, such a policy would focus its attention on the actions of the rich rather than punishing the poor, not unlike prostitution laws that seek to prosecute those who seek out, perpetuate, and profit from exploitative systems rather than in persecuting sex workers themselves. Ptoxocratic values could easily be defended by legal measures, though again, these are not likely to come into effect without a ptoxocratic government in place.

One might say that all of this sounds expensive and unwieldy, that society is better to leave financial eligibility requirements out of office-seeking and continue in the current direction. My rebuttal to this argument is simple: rich rulers are incredibly expensive. The security and travel costs of a wealthy chief executive who chooses to play golf at their private estate 998 miles away each weekend costs the taxpayer far more than would government offices of accountability each year. Moreover, the rich as policymakers regularly make decisions that are bad for most citizens, funneling wealth into the pockets of the few rather than the wallets of the many. I argue that a ptoxocratic government would be cheaper and thriftier without sacrificing any dignity or integrity of office. The financial lives of the poor are already examined without dignity. My assumption is that with greater access to power, that ptoxocratic leaders would not mind having their financial lives examined under eligibility requirements, as there is little story to tell. It is the rich who would most burden these bureaucrats tasked with accountability, as they ever do.

Upon raising this set of problems, one notices once again the translation of the power of wealth into the power of politics, and the ways in which this translation is, outside ptoxocratic systems, taken to be a given. Immediately within these critiques one notices an implicit argument for the idea of ptoxocracy itself within the questions laid forth previously. The idea that wealthy individuals recognize that there is vast potential for future enrichment within powerful structures of governance acknowledges the implicit danger of the coupling of power and wealth. The desperation of wealthy individuals to gain or maintain power speaks more loudly of the magnetism between wealth and power than it does about the difficulty of creating procedural restraints and bureaucratic checks and balances to maintain justice. The question itself, therefore, amounts to something of a condemnation of the allure of wealth, that it tempts individuals toward the acquisition of more and more, thereby depleting resources and potential of the poor.

Compensation of Officeholders

The issue of compensation for officeholders within ptoxocracy arrives at a particularly thorny question: Public servants are well paid in some places—wouldn't those salaries render them ineligible for office?

In 2018 voters of San Diego overwhelmingly adopted Measure L, a plan to increase the salaries of elected members of the city council over a five-year time frame. The measure also set in place automatic annual salary increases, so that local politicians wouldn't have to burden themselves with the political fallout of requesting them. Where a city council member made roughly $75,000 in 2018, by 2023 they made about $173,000. According to an article published by *The San Diego Union-Tribune*, the logic behind this decision is simple: the city was having a difficult time encouraging talented potential leaders to run for office, given the potential pay cuts they might endure through such a term. In the words of the *Union-Tribune*, "Supporters have long hailed the measure for sharply boosting the quality of candidates running for elected office in the city, especially council seats. Now, lawyers, doctors and other professionals can run for council without taking massive pay cuts."[5] So, yes, under the current system of salary increases and wages, such a position would absolutely render a ptoxocratic leader ineligible within a year.

The logic of these wage increases is fascinating when examined through the analytical lens of ptoxocracy. Essentially the logic of these pay raises supports one of the earlier points made about our existing non-ptoxocratic forms of government: the only persons encouraged (or perhaps desired) as candidates for governmental office are already wealthy persons whose interests are taken as society's best interests. The current system prioritizes those who have a stake in the well-being of the rich and deprioritizes those who do not. True, a trained and practicing attorney is a helpful person to have on a city council, as the *Union-Tribune* article points out. City officials constantly deal in matters where legal expertise is not only helpful, but essential. Yet it does not take much to see how the upward cycle of wage growth continues to depress the interests of the poor, how those now-enticed members of the governing class might continue to hold less and less interest in the actual realities of the poor, since they themselves are not from among these classes and communities.

So yes, a balance in negotiating fair wages and ptoxocracy would absolutely need to be struck. Again, this seems to be something that could be overcome with little sophistication. More important, however, is identifying the perpetual logic of statecraft in practice among us today, which is taken as a given among citizens when considering the relationship of wealth to power, that continues to prioritize the wealthy over the poor.

5. Garrick, "San Diego Elected Officials," para. 7.

INTERROGATING PTOXOCRACY
The Challenge of Good Governance

There is an odd sleight of hand when dealing in class distinction that to be identified as one class rather than another is to somehow create disparities or inequalities. The idea of ptoxocracy is not that the poor are any more naturally inclined toward the wielding of governmental authority than the rich. While it is true that they have a stake in the poor, rendering them, perhaps, more qualified to make judgments to bring forth just policies for a wider number of persons within society at large, the fact of their poverty does not render them any more naturally inclined to power than the rich. This is more a question of bias than actuality. The bias revealed lies in the unexamined translation of wealth into power, the idea that one who has created wealth must necessarily be a good statesman. In other words, we must deal with the belief that businessmen make great leaders. This, now, takes us back to the mythology of the rich ruling class, an idea that falsely equivocates the accumulation of goods and money with a capacity for governance. Indeed, the rich make great CEOs whose focus is the perpetual increase of shareholder value. They are even excellent at seeking opportunities that can bring about the flourishing of other human beings through the creation of job opportunities. They are also good at maximizing profits by underpaying, undervaluing, and cutting vulnerable staff dispassionately. But all of this is beside the point. Governance, by its nature, isn't profit-seeking. Those who believe that the aim of statecraft is the maximization of shareholder value are those persons who ought to be ineligible for office, as they tend to make terrible decisions on behalf of the community. If good governance is characterized by a modicum of peace, the absence of violence, and equality among citizens, then it is uncertain whether the rich would receive a good grade to this point. The sooner that we remember that what rich, democratically elected rulers have in common with despots, authoritarians, and tyrants is wealth itself, the sooner we realize the primary argument for ptoxocracy.

The International Problem

Given the intricate relationships among nations in the twenty-first century, as well as the dominance of wealthy interests in the political mechanisms of other nations, one must interrogate the extent to which other nations would tolerate a ptoxocratic nation in principle. Again, what a fascinating criticism of wealth lies implicit in this question, the idea that wealthy interests look out for one another across national boundaries, and that all wealthy share a loathing for sharing power. Yet, historically speaking, this is not unimaginable, and the realities of international politics demand historical recognition. Emigre nobles petitioned for just such a form of counter-revolutionary change during the French Revolution throughout the courts of monarchical Europe. A more charitable restatement of this problem might be that the rich in one nation most easily find business and commerce partners in the wealthy citizens of another nation, and that ptoxocracy may damage the capacity of one nation's wealthy to do business with another. Yet another restatement of this problem could find parallel in Cold War geopolitical politics, that one nation's economics or systems of governance implicitly threaten others of a too-divergent character. To the latter iteration of the problem the only response is, in fact, yes. Yes, nations with diverging characters of governance will find one another intolerable on some level. Citizens of the United States will ever scratch their heads confusedly at the monarchical democratic system of Great Britain. These, however, are much closer in form than, say, the governments of the United States and North Korea, and the very shape of their governance is a source of mutual enmity. Ptoxocracy would almost certainly irk some nations more than others, no matter who implemented it. Moreover, some nations will take ptoxocracy as weakness rather than an expression of greater strength, which it indeed may be. A ptoxocratic government behind the wheel of a nation whose business and government interests were previously harmonious would almost certainly do things differently. In some cases, we can imagine that ptoxocratic leaders would choose different pathways toward peacemaking and governance than their rich forebears since ptoxocratic leaders would now hold meaningful interests in the lives of the poor, who are often most affected by clashes between world powers. This would frustrate former allies and other nations, to be sure.

What this criticism implies, however, is that statecraft is relatively static under non-ptoxocratic governance and may be put under particular duress under ptoxocracy. Yet all states, nearly by definition, find one another abhorrent, and jostle for power through the illusions of weakness. This is what keeps boundaries intact, and governments separate from one another. The ptoxocratic state has the same means to participate in global affairs as a pre-ptoxocratic government might have done. It is true that the relationships between this ptoxocratic government, its allies and adversaries, would shift due to a realignment of interests, but in some respects, this is, in fact, the point of ptoxocracy. The rich, to this point, have not accomplished a means of human governance that prioritizes the well-being of the poor and marginalized, neither have they been the arbiters of peace and tranquility. The history of war, colonization, exploitation, human enslavement, and ecological disaster belongs to the wealthy rulers. We cannot be confident that the poor might do much better as leaders, but it is a curious thing that the record of rich rulers would not give us pause in and of itself.

Ptoxocracy and Violence

Another problem consists in understanding the historical relationship between wealth and state violence, especially in the rise of so-called warlords in nations with weak governments. The question raised here points to the ways in which wealth and power continue to draw toward one another even when political power has been taken out of the equation—that is, by forming a kind of alternative state by way of their wealth. The history of Central and South American politics, for example, is riddled with examples of just such a tension between the weakened executive branch and independent *caudillos*, or wealthy warlords whose wealth funds access to weapons. In such a case, one can imagine something comparable to fiefdoms emerging within ptoxocratic society, a nation built up of wealthy individuals who look after their own security interests within a given sphere of influence. Further, one imagines that within this context the government would weaken significantly, and that informal, but significantly less just and more violent plutocratic systems would take its place. This argument purports that the wealthy will find other ways to gain power, not completely encompassing but involving power over violence, regardless of whomever oversees the government, or however a given democracy's citizens decide on policies of control. In other words, this critique insists that the wealthy will seek to create a parallel state in which they are the arbiters of justice, policymakers, and executives, and hold a capacity for arming individuals to protect the myopia of their interests.

Mike Duncan, in the summary of his *Revolutions* podcast, notes that one way to define a sovereign is to recognize it as the body that holds a "monopoly on the legitimate use of force."[6] This is exactly the power given over to the poor in ptoxocracy. Do not imagine that ptoxocracy means

6. Duncan, "Appendix 10."

the diminishment of government capacity, or an unwillingness to exercise force to protect a nation's citizens, territory, and interests. Rather, these are exactly the tools of government held in the hands of policymakers and executives in a ptoxocratic state. Ptoxocracy does not imagine a state without violence, however morally reprehensible one finds state violence. Rather, it asserts that the monopolization of violence is better placed in the hands of the poor than the rich, since the poor have fewer reasons to trivially enact state violence.

By subverting the will of ptoxocratic democracy through the creation of a subset of new power brokers, this counterargument amounts to no less than a plutocratic restitution. A monopoly on violence is exactly the kind of actual power given over to the poor in ptoxocracy—that is, a ptoxocratic society sees that the only citizens fit to hold this power are the poor. The rich have proven themselves incapable of holding this power. History shows a procession of rich rulers from Octavian to Jefferson who, at the helm of government, use the government to further their own private interests. Thomas Jefferson, a wealthy white slave-owner, was never going to allow the disillusion of slavery as president, as it would directly compete with the heart of his most profitable enterprises. Rather, it took a nonslaveholding Northern lawyer to finally break through the entrenchment of those interest and end chattel slavery in the United States. Thus are the rich incapable of holding this monopoly: we can only speculate that Thomas Jefferson would have employed the strength of his nation to protect his slaveholding interests.

Now, a counterpoint could be raised. What if a certain wealthy person were to buy off whole sectors of the government's monopoly on violence and use it against the state? In this case the rich amass their wealth to purchase existing assets from the armed forces (personnel, tools, weapons, expertise) and use it against their nation. This is a problem of insurgency in general, not ptoxocracy. Any state that cannot handle its own military and properly equip, supply, and pay for it has problems that surpass this argument. Ptoxocratic rulers would have all the tax dollars available to their wealthy pre-ptoxocratic counterparts (likely more, as they may enact tax policy that serves and enforces fair tax laws) at their disposal. Why would we assume that poor leaders within a government must have a poor government? To the contrary! Nothing in ptoxocracy means that the state shouldn't continue to collect tax revenue and hold a monopoly on violence.

The root of this criticism might be a suspicion that the poor would turn out to be more lenient on crime than their wealthy counterparts, or less effective in executing, enacting, and adjudicating laws. This suspicion arises, in part, from an unexamined prejudice that most criminals are poor, as if, once again, poverty was a result of a logical, meritocratic society in which poverty and unintelligence were correlated. While an unverified assumption indeed, we might spend a little time here parsing this question out to help ourselves. I imagine that the criticism's logic goes that the more lenient (or less effective) a nation is on crime, the less capacity it has in holding off violent challenges to its monopoly on violence. Or, that the poor might target the wealthy through state violence (again, back to one of our first problems), or neglect to protect them and therefore give rise to a state where private security becomes the norm for wealthy persons.

To begin untangling these questions, we first see that it's true that the poor might implement policies and law enforcement techniques that less-adversely affect marginalized communities. This is a benefit, not a loss, in ptoxocracy. One might say that this is, in fact, something of the point of the whole project. A ptoxocratic government would likely be a more representative government, and there's no doubt that policymakers would work hard to ensure the communities from which they emerged have adequate capacity to live harmoniously without fear of police violence or suspicious government actors. But the inference of lenience is a dubious one, as is any bias of capacity to adjudicate, enact, and execute law. The rich are no better at these tasks of government than the poor, and no more intelligent or prepared to execute the matters at hand. A state must hold its monopoly on violence, or else it ceases to be the state. The interests of the nation, not just the poor, would be lost if a grip on this monopoly were to give way. A belief that rich persons understand the mechanisms of violence better than the poor speaks badly of the rich, and betrays an ad hominem line of attack against the poor, rather than a systemic, thoughtful attack on ptoxocracy.

The Place of Wealth in Ptoxocracy

Wealth in ptoxocratic society translates into just about everything it can buy in non-ptoxocratic societies with one exception: the power of wealth has no political purchasing power. The Political-Science-101-level rejection of Marxism is completely ineffective against the simple solution of ptoxocratic democracy. A citizen of ptoxocracy may either be rich or powerful, but never both.

Toward this question we can say two things: ptoxocracy can only be achieved by legal, nonvindictive methods. The will of the voters has final say in matters of elected officials, and the will of the voters (in such circumstances) would express itself by way of disqualifying the rich from power. Just as we already disqualify some potential leaders from power given their history as lawmakers, ethical conduct, and so on, so too can the will of the voters express itself likewise toward the rich. It is not unfair. To the second point, the rich have had over two millennia to prove themselves as great leaders. Their de facto status as the ruling class has provided ample opportunity to prove that rich leaders make for great leaders. Yet one might argue that the presence of war, poverty, segregation, racism, ecological disasters, corruption, and exploitation of the poor persist as realities which our present slate of leaders are unwilling to tackle. If the rich were inherently good or inherently best at ruling, as the mythology of the rich ruling class would suggest, would we not see an alleviation of poverty each year to some degree? Would we not see some meaningful action toward climate justice? As it stands, we do not, and cannot, so long as the rich are in power. It is not in their interests to take meaningful action against these: it is in their interests to keep these systems in place.

CONCLUSION

The mythology of the rich ruling class is problematic, but its conclusion and a hidden mythology lodged within its own logic, which I would call the *mythology of the deserving poor*, is quadruply so. "Poverty [in America]," writes Matthew Desmond, "is an injury, a taking. Tens of millions of Americans do not end up poor by mistake of history or personal conduct. Poverty persists because some wish and will it to."[7] Poverty in America is not just a given, it's an intentional one, brought about at all levels of power through the incapacity and unwillingness of leaders to solve this particular uniquely American expression of the problem. This is also Greg Boyle's point, that poverty is the system working exactly as it is intended to work: the rich stay rich and the poor stay poor, he says, because we (and again, I am careful to include myself among the rich *we* here) intentionally allow for it to function that way, or at the very least because we unconsciously

---

7. Desmond, *Poverty, by America*, 40.

benefit from this structure. Until the rich ruler holds a meaningful stake, a vested and actual interest in the well-being of the poor, they will remain incapable of enacting policy that could have a meaningful impact in the lives of the poor outside of mere charity. Until we sever the connection between power and wealth, the rich ruler will never have a stake in the lives of the poor, for their stake in the lives of the wealthy will always be both more consequential and more important.

Ptoxocracy imagines what has previously been unexplored political terrain—that is, the decoupling of wealth and power. While we have language that expresses rule by certain persons or a certain class of persons, such as the rich (plutocracy), rule by the old (gerontocracy), and even rule by those most worthy (meritocracy), no such word exists in the English lexicon for rule by the poor (ptoxocracy). One wonders why language has never accounted for the possibility of rule by the poor. Those arguing against ptoxocracy must either do so from evidence (i.e., the poor are incapable of ruling), from history (i.e., it's never been a possibility), or divine intent (i.e., God has ordained certain persons to rule over others, all of whom happen to be or become rich). It is regarding this latter argument that the Christian tradition, as evidenced by the Gospels in the witness of the earthly ministry of Jesus, could have much to say. Jesus clearly sees a way to bridge the great chasm between rich and poor.

5

Blessed Are the *Ptoxoi*

Listen, my beloved brothers and sisters. Has not God chosen the poor in the world to be rich in faith and to be heirs of the kingdom that he has promised to those who love him?

— James 2:5

One of the most difficult tasks of constructive theology is to ensure that the image of God reflected in our work together mirrors what we know of divine reality, and not our own image. It's easy to fashion an image of God that looks a lot more like our own interests, ideas, and perspectives, than it is to confront the often-disquieting truth of God's image reflected in Scripture. As the old warning among pastors goes, if your image of Jesus votes like you, has the same enemies as you, and calls the same people friends as you, it's likely that you are not worshipping a true image of God, but an image of yourself. Faith calls us to imagine and listen to the ways that God is speaking, not our own egos.

So, it is with this warning clanging in my ears that I make the following claim: Jesus was a ptoxocrat.

Admittedly, this is an ahistorical claim, and not one that Jesus makes explicitly. Yet we may examine the political philosophy of Jesus as predominantly ptoxocratic in nature from three angles. First, with an examination of political authority, and the ways that Jesus does and does not ordain political authority to certain groups—namely, in his blessing of the poor as inheriting the dominion of God. We then bolster this claim by acknowledging the centrality of the *ptoxoi* to the Gospels, helping us see the supreme priority that Jesus gives to these within the scope of his earthly ministry. This is what Gustavo Gutiérrez calls God's "preferential option for the poor."[1] Finally, we examine Jesus's complex relationship to wealth, one which preserves divine love for the wealthy without authorizing their domination over the poor. The constellation that emerges from this set of examinations appears ptoxocratic in form. The aim of this chapter is to make it clear that this ptoxocracy is not an invention of the twenty-first century. A perfectly clear vision of this project has been hiding in plain sight for people of faith for over two millennia, with roots long centered in the Hebrew prophets and calls for justice for the poor.

PTOXOCRACY AND ESCHATOLOGY

It is amazing that the rich have managed consistently to twist and mangle Scripture so badly over two millennia as to lend credibility to their claim to earthly leadership that resembles aristocracy or its devolution, oligarchy. How Jesus, who, in his own words, was anointed and sent "to preach good news to the *ptoxoi*" (Luke 4:18b; translation mine) might speak these words as one of the first acts of his ministry, then go on to divinely authorize an earthly economic elite to rule over society stretches belief beyond credulity. And yet the wealthy have nevertheless sought authority by way of church doctrine, Scripture, and traditions. As we have seen already, kings and queens, emperors and dictators have claimed legal right by divine authorization by citing psalms, epistles, historical scripture, tradition, and even the Gospels. Citing divine authorization of the Davidic monarchy—willfully forgetting God's lament of the tyrannical tendencies of kings in 1 Samuel—the rich point to their own authority both in and as God's law. Rule by divine right is not an invention of Christianity, but it is an invention that the wealthy have sought to read into Christian history, and one that has devalued poor citizens.

It wasn't until very recently, for example, that my own denomination, the Evangelical Lutheran Church in America, officially repudiated the doctrine of discovery in a vote by the church's representative body. This is a doctrine which "originate[d] with 15th century Papal Bulls that were issued by the Vatican and implemented by Monarchies, sanctioning the brutal Conquest and Colonization of non-Christians who were deemed 'enemies

---

1. Gutiérrez, *Theology of Liberation*, 156.

of Christ' in Africa and the Americas."[2] In a nutshell, toxic ideologies of racism were codified into church doctrine and used as a means of domination over the peoples of the New World. The doctrine of discovery gave divine authorization to the "discoverers" (read: abuse, oppression, genocidal work) over those who had been "discovered." Repudiation of this doctrine is an important step in making things right, though it is not the end of our work. The damage of this doctrine is deep, and the work undoing these wrongs continues.

History tells the story repeatedly of rulers as authorized by God to govern a certain people in a certain place. Cherry-picked Bible verses do little in the way of acknowledging Jesus's constant attention to the poor and marginalized in society, how the rest of his ministry (and the Hebrew tradition from which it is born) quite specifically points to God's particular concern for those economically outside the halls of power. When usurped as means of authorizing authority by the rich, the context in which the verses reside is also missing.

One can seem to legitimize nearly any expression of power through the contortion of biblical interpretation. The task in this chapter is less to categorize the historical grievances of the marginalized than to let another set of scriptural references inform a new structure—namely, one that prioritizes all children of God, including the *ptoxoi*. This form is ptoxocracy, and the foundation of its divine authority rests in Jesus's Sermon on the Plain in Luke 6.

Jesus authorizes earthly ruling authority of the poor by way of articulating an image of the kingdom of God to come. In the words of Günther Bornkamm, "God's future is God's call to the present, and the present is the time of decision in the light of God's future."[3] Theologians call this *eschatology*, or *eschatological hope*. Justo González notes the ways that observing God's far-off kingdom—that is, what life in heaven might look like—can inform the ways that we act now. "In order to recover the full dimension of eschatological hope, we need to recover the full dimension of the future."[4] González helps us to see the import and challenge of the future kingdom of God, so often articulated by Jesus, and illustrates what he means here by way of an example:

2. Doctrine of Discovery Project, "What is the Doctrine of Discovery?"
3. Bornkamm, *Jesus of Nazareth*, 93.
4. González, *Luke*, 241.

The future *causes* much of the present. I am now writing these words because they will be published; and they will be published because they will be read. Certainly, such hopes may never be fulfilled; but still it is out of them that these words are written, and without that hope they would not be written.

The other side of the same coin is that our faith in the future is either corroborated or belied by our present actions. If I say that I expect this book to be published, but do not write it, no one will believe that I really expect the book to be published. If I claim belief in a coming kingdom of peace, love, and justice, and meanwhile do not practice peace, love, and justice, all my protestations of faith will avail nothing.[5]

Near the end of his recent work of systematic theology, *Christianity as a Way of Life*, Kevin Hector writes of the difficulties for theologians in writing and speaking of life after death. "I sometimes tell students," he says, "that the best way to handle the doctrine of last things,"—that is, eschatology—"is to follow the example of Thomas Aquinas and Karl Barth, and *perform* the doctrine (by dying before completing one's system), rather than *write* about it."[6] I find myself constantly in the particularly uncomfortable position of attending to these questions as a pastor, without any option (or desire) to perform eschatology. Questions about life after death arise all the time, in attending to grieving widowers, fielding Bible study questions by parishioners in close readings of Gospel texts, or by curious fourteen-year-old confirmation students who have been watching NBC's *The Good Place*. After years of these questions, though, I must admit that each time they come up I wish I, too, could perform the doctrine, or in the very least that I could just hide behind my office desk.

Some of these questions arise out of a sense of identity, others out of fear, and still others because the questioner suspects it might be a weak point of church doctrine or pastoral wisdom. To the latter sense, I don't think they're incorrect: too many well-meaning pastors have supplied flimsy, whimsical, or evasive answers to these questions too frequently, and parishioners are right to call us out. But that's not to say the questions are not of genuine significance to the person asking them. For instance, the grieving widower asked about heaven, it turned out, because he was ready to move on to a new relationship with another partner later in life but wondered whether he'd face an uncomfortable eschatological reality.

5. González, *Luke*, 241–242; italics mine.
6. Hector, *Christianity as a Way of Life*, 242.

The confirmand wondered about heaven because he worried that being gay meant he'd find himself in hell, which, as it turns out, another Christian classmate told him at school. The Bible study group wondered about questions of heaven and hell because they had been reading Jesus's statements about the nearness of the kingdom of God in Matthew's Gospel and had never, until now, thought of heaven as anything outside a future great hereafter. The way we respond to questions about life after death matter, and listeners deserve serious, loving pastoral attention to these concerns. How we speak and imagine the kingdom of God in the eschatological sense affects the present, which is exactly González's point. The stakes are high, and we ignore them at our peril. These questions come up all the time, and to Hector's point, avoiding them leaves us in a precarious position as human beings, however tempting it is to hide behind our desks.

I hear some fear when a parishioner asks these questions, and rightly so. What if I learn that the goal of life, or the good life, was missed, and it's too late to change course? What if I receive a rejection notice at the pearly gates because of my actions on earth? What if my loved one receives a rejection notice? These are consequential questions to ask, and faithful folks are right to ask them. Nevertheless, I usually wish I had a bigger desk when they do, if only because I know how consequential these questions are pastorally.

Beyond getting the answers wrong, and the inherent existential anxiety of that problem, are some of the bodily or physical implications of the questions themselves: in merely asking about a place called heaven we imply that place to be a thing of substance. Will I have a body in eternal life? Will my earthly relationships still exist intact, reconciled, or broken? What will it look like? What will I remember? Will my sins be remembered, forgotten, or forgiven? These are just a few of the important questions I get on a regular basis. While the Christian tradition affirms the validity of these questions, the answers vary widely. That said, there is some agreement in the answers given, and there are enough great theologians who have not performed eschatology that we can do better than provide flimsy responses.

One of these is Thomas Long. Long's *Accompany Them with Singing* is a piece of pastoral theology that argues for a return to traditional Christian funeral practices from out of his eschatological theology. Long, aside from making this argument, spends nearly as much time articulating a theology of death precisely for these pastoral moments, knowing how often and how seriously they arise in the daily course of pastoring. Long's theology, while helpful for several reasons, stresses what is generally true of the Christian tradition—namely, the importance of *bodily* resurrection. He writes, "The bodily resurrection of Jesus—so troubling to philosophers, so perplexing to scientists, so repulsive to Gnostics—is a crucial claim, but not a crudely literalistic one."[7] Without going too deeply into Long's excellent work, it suffices to say that his pastoral theology of death articulates the singular importance and centrality of bodies to resurrection. "[The risen Jesus] is in history and time, and his body is familiar and recognizable, bearing yet the wounds of his cruel death."[8] Again, here we see Long's relatively orthodox stress on bodies after death—that is, in the fleshy stuff of human life contained (or at least included within) the idea of eternal life. Bodies are central to life on earth, and they are central to life in eternity. I can't recommend his work highly enough and am grateful that neither Long nor Hector chose to perform their eschatologies before getting them down on paper (or hiding behind their desks).

While I won't go any further down the road of these eschatological works, the theological stress on bodies gives us pause. It might seem silly to ask, but if eternal life contains the reality of human flesh, does it also contain digestive realities? In other words, do humans process food via their digestive tracts, including the need to eject nonessential waste? Jesus ate fish after the resurrection, but did his organs process it into energy? Awkwardly, we must ask, are there toilets in heaven? If the answer to that question is yes, then we're left with another question. As in the case of earthly realities dealing with human waste (i.e., sewer treatment plants, sewers, regulations, etc.), who or what deliberative body oversees the maintenance of and creation of these? I'm teasing out what Long might consider "crudely literalistic" questions here that may seem silly or trivial, but the conundrum posed by Christian emphasis on bodies in eternal life persists, nevertheless. If Christian theology emphasizes bodily realities of eternal life, then what, if any, bodily realities of human life do these bodies entail? On earth we know that these questions are answered in large part by the municipalities—that is, authorities of ruling political power. Does that mean that there are rulers in heaven who also oversee the necessary upkeep of all that flows from the realities of human bodies? If I take questions of eschatology from widowers and confirmands to be important because they influence our lives here and now, then I see no reason that questions of

---

7. Long, *Accompany Them with Singing*, 43.
8. Long, *Accompany Them with Singing*, 45.

how bodies function in eternal life shouldn't also be of importance. True, thinking about toilets in heaven feels a little off-putting, yet it is precisely the off-putting realities of this world that give rise to the need for ruling powers.

Jesus gives sermons in the Gospels of both Matthew and Luke. Famously known as the Sermon on the Mount and Sermon on the Plain respectively, Jesus delivers within these his Beatitudes, or blessings. Interestingly, interpreters throughout history seem to emphasize one side of these beatific statements over the other, as in Luke's "blessed are you who are poor, for yours is the kingdom of God" (Luke 6:20). Interpreters will often lay the emphasis of this text on interpreting what is meant to *bless* the poor. In her recent work *The Beatitudes Through the Ages*, scholar Rebekah Eklund takes readers through the historical development of such interpretations, noting the ways that this verse is handled, a task that is made even more difficult by its parallel verse in Matthew's Gospel, in which "the poor in spirit" is written instead of simply "the poor." Eklund does a great job tracing its interpretation through early church leaders, who tend to emphasize humility and total reliance on God. By contrast, she notes that today's interpreters tend to see Luke's earthly emphasis on poverty at issue. Despite justifiably dedicating many pages to the emphasis of the first half of this verse and the prominent theologians who have taken pains in interpreting it through history, it's not until late in her chapter on this work that she sees the second half—that is, the *poor* as inheriting the kingdom of God. She writes, "Most commentators see the possession of the kingdom of God through a 'now and not yet' lens, as a matter of partial fulfillment now and completion in the next age: 'both grace here, and glory hereafter.'"[9]

What would it mean to hold the second half of Luke's blessing as an answer to the eschatological questions, questions that arise from the orthodox implication of bodily resurrection, however silly they feel? That is, what would it mean to emphasize not only the first, but the second half of Jesus's blessing? The ramifications are enormous to our project: namely, that the poor rule the kingdom of God. If this is the case, then it would seem to be precisely the kind of divine authorization of ruling power that the rich erroneously claim.

Jesus is constantly walking the tension between what some theologians refer to as the *now* and the *not yet*, For instance, the first words Jesus speaks aloud in Mark's Gospel are, "The time is fulfilled, and the kingdom of God

---

9. Eklund, *Beatitudes Through the Ages*, 95.

has come near; repent, and believe in the good news" (Mark 1:15). This initial preaching would seem to indicate that with the arrival of Jesus, the kingdom has arrived now—that is, in the present moment for those hearing the proclamation. Yet John's Gospel records a seemingly contradictory statement in the form of Jesus's retort to Pilate's accusation of his claiming the authority of a king: "My kingdom," says Jesus, "does not belong to this world. If my kingdom belonged to this world, my followers would be fighting to keep me from being handed over to the Jews. But as it is, my kingdom is not from here" (John 18:36). In this scene Jesus seems to be making the opposite claim, that the kingdom of God (taken as what he means by "my" kingdom) is not yet, or at least not of a present moment. Rather than taking these seeming contradictions as proof of internal confusion or incongruity of Jesus's theology, we can deduce an intentional and productive tension between these statements that emerges between and alongside the now and not yet of God's kingdom. In fact, it is this very tension that both authorizes the ptoxocratic and allows for salvation history as a continually unfolding reality within the constraints of both time and space. As González reminds us, the realities of the not yet (that is, the kingdom of God) are intended to inform our actions in the now, while they are also meant to look toward the not yet in hope.

Theologians call this the *prolyptic present*, a productive tension between the future reality of God's kingdom and its present reality, a tension that is mutually informing of both the now and the not yet. One place where this is clear is in Jesus's first preaching opportunity as attested in Luke's Gospel: Jesus points his ministry not toward the political elite of the world, but to the *ptoxoi* (Luke 4). This identifies his audience, his people, the centrality of intention in the now. The coming (not yet) dominion of God will exist for their sake, he says, for the *ptoxoi*. What follows is fascinating, connecting the story of God's concern for the poor and marginalized known in the prophets to his own ministry, which bears retelling in full since it so clearly delineates a connection between the embodied mission of God in Jesus the Christ and the *ptoxoi*—that is, the materially poor.

> Then Jesus, in the power of the Spirit, returned to Galilee, and a report about him spread through all the surrounding region. He began to teach in their synagogues and was praised by everyone.
> When he came to Nazareth, where he had been brought up, he went to the synagogue on the Sabbath day, as was his custom. He stood up to read, and the scroll of the prophet Isaiah was given

to him. He unrolled the scroll and found the place where it was written:

> "The Spirit of the Lord is upon me,
> because he has anointed me
> to bring good news to the poor.
>   He has sent me to proclaim release to the captives
> and recovery of sight to the blind,
> to set free those who are oppressed,
>   to proclaim the year of the Lord's favor."
>
> And he rolled up the scroll, gave it back to the attendant, and sat down. The eyes of all in the synagogue were fixed on him. Then he began to say to them, "Today this scripture has been fulfilled in your hearing." (Luke 4:14–21)

The first words out of his mouth are a proclamation, that God has anointed Jesus to bring good news to the *ptoxoi*. In the end of the reading we hear that it has been fulfilled in the hearing of those who were present (as it is fulfilled in the now of our hearing, even as Isaiah first spoke it as a not yet). This is the good news that he has come to embody, the good news that God has decided to bring to God's dominion—that is, all of us. It will implicate all of us, yet the pronouncement of God's nearness is of supreme importance for the *ptoxoi*. What sense would it make if the consequence of this pronouncement were the divine right of the *plusioi* in attaining ruling power?

Matthew and Mark give us a slightly different account of Jesus's first act of preaching, when Jesus pronounces that the kingdom of God—that is, the dominion of God—has drawn near. In proclaiming this nearness of God's kingdom, Jesus means his own body dwelling and walking on earth. The very body of Christ walking among us ushers in a new age of God's dominion over the earth. It is an inaugurated age, as we see in his exchanges with Satan in the wilderness, that explicitly rejects the ways of the world as he finds it. In fact, the first time this word *basileus* (dominion, kingdom) is used in Luke's Gospel, Jesus explicitly rejects dominion over earthly kingdoms in precisely the way that the kings and rulers of the world wield it—that is, as domination of the wealthy over the poor. Luke is clear, moreover, that such coupling of wealth and political power is rejected by Jesus precisely because it is not of the kingdom of God, that it is, in fact, a form of idolatry contrary to God's desire. In the exchange, Luke's telling explicitly links this form of domination with Satan: "Then the devil led

[Jesus] up and showed him in an instant all the kingdoms of the world. And the devil said to him, 'To you I will give all this authority and their glory, for it has been given over to me, and I give it to anyone I please. If you, then, will worship me, it will all be yours'" (Luke 4:5–7). When rejecting the connection between ruler and ownership, ruling and domination, Jesus is also rejecting worship of the devil. In short, Jesus engages the reality of earthly structures of human power (the now he encounters) while simultaneously pronouncing God's not yet as the aim of his project. He not only rejects the forms of human domination encountered in the earth's kingdoms but condemns them outrightly as antithetical to God's own kingdom. In other words, God's kingdom does not link wealth and political power; in fact, such a linkage is the very fact that renders it demonic—that is, antithetical to God's kingdom.

All this is to say that the eschatological blessing of the poor in Jesus's Sermon on the Plain serves as divine-right authority for ptoxocracy. Ironically, plutocratic rulers have managed to do this for thousands of years, serving to bolster their own claims of ruling authority by way of Scripture. If there is any claim to authority to be had for any human form of governance, it is ptoxocratic in origin, not plutocratic. In a sense, Jesus's words of blessing to the poor function as a timely warning to present listeners, not a prediction of some distant future. Theologian Osvaldo Vena, writing for preachers pouring over the Beatitudes in a cycle of Matthew's Gospel, writes, "The implication of Jesus blessing the poor, the marginalized, is not that they should be happy in their deprivation, for even though they may be poor materially they surely are rich spiritually! No. It is more an indictment on the society of the time for having forgotten its responsibility toward the neighbor. It is a warning to God's people. It is a call to accountability, for if God blesses the ones that you curse, there is something fundamentally wrong with your theology."[10] In other words, the blessing of the poor by Jesus functions as a present and urgent call to action now. That *now* can be read as the now of Jesus's listeners, but it can also be read as a now to present listeners of every age, a source of authority when debating forms and structures of society that may or may not serve the greatest number of persons.

As we have seen thus far, our present form of government and those which have come before tend to employ some form of the mythology of the rich ruling class as either a basis for their authority or an explanation of it.

---

10. Vena, "Commentary on Matthew 5:1–12," para. 12.

Spoken plainly, in these systems, the rich rule. Yet, in the biblical imagination of the Gospels, quite the contrary is true. In the dominion of God, the poor rule. Luke's Gospel states it most clearly when Jesus preaches, "Blessed are the poor, for yours is the dominion of God" (translation mine).

On Blessing

A brief theology of blessing may be helpful as we dive into exactly what Jesus means when he claims that the *ptoxoi* are blessed as those who rule over his dominion. It would be a mischaracterization of blessing, as some have done, to associate blessing or blessedness with material goods, as if these goods are a sign of blessing. To bless, rather, is to remember and recognize the source from which something came. It is not a verb, a spell or charm cast upon someone to bestow special honor. To bless is to recognize God as the source of all that is known, including the source of the goodness known in the subject of a blessing. To bless is to recognize the image of God within what is at hand. One scholar translates Jesus's use of *blessing* here (*makarion*) as "Godlike in happiness."[11] Jesus's blessing of the poor makes no sense if that which is blessed is that which is prosperous or wealthy. To bless, instead, is to hold up to a mirror and remember the imprint of the image of God. Happiness for the Godlike could be something delayed or in the far-off future, but this same word is applied thrice to detail the condition of those experiencing a present reality and coupled with the word *now*. "Godlike in happiness" are you who are hungering now, Jesus says, just after mirroring the Godlike in happy who are poor. The point is that the quality of blessedness conveyed here by Jesus, whether Godlike in happiness or simply mirroring a divine reality or even taken as material prosperity (which it is not), is its quality of immediacy, or nearness. Greek grammar is clear: this is a present blessing.

This Godlike blessedness, as it turns out, is for a particular set of people (the *ptoxoi*), and it is intended for both the now and the not yet. "Blessed are you *ptoxoi*, yours is the dominion of God" (translation mine). Given the ways that the lives of the *ptoxoi* are lived in stark contrast to this statement, the pronouncement is either a joke, or an articulation of profound political consequence: the poor are the only ones authorized by God to rule the dominion of God. Remembering González's explanation of how God's future reality serves to inform our present reality, we can thus

11. Swanson, *Provoking the Gospel of Luke*, 262.

interpret Jesus's preaching in the following way: This is my blessing, this is the reality that I would see mirrored in the world of the now, that the poor would rule the earth, just as they rule in God's not-yet kingdom. In such a world, Jesus goes on to say, the hungry will eat and the ones weeping now will have a condition of life in which they will laugh. In a world oriented in this way, a world turned upside down in fact, the poor will eat and be satisfied. Mary sang that in such a world the rich would be sent away empty, but empty of what? Framed in ptoxocratic terms, empty of the capacity to translate their wealth into political power.

This is the theological center of ptoxocracy as rooted deeply in Jewish and Christian Scripture: that the poor will eat and be satisfied. In the dominion of God, that is both in heaven and on earth, the poor are the only ones authorized by God to rule over others. All other forms of government supposedly authorized by God are fraudulent both on earth and in heaven.

JESUS AND THE PTOXOI

To paraphrase William Sloane Coffin, every theological project that takes Scripture as a source of authority will ultimately be a selectively literalist account.[12] My form of selective literalistic reading takes Jesus's blessing of the poor as the basis of an earthly structure of human political power for the here and now—namely, ptoxocracy. Acknowledging this, however, it is difficult to read the Gospels without meeting the *ptoxoi* at every turn. I have always been fascinated by the number of warnings about wealth that Jesus issues, and the refusal of literalist readings into these by wealthy persons. While literalist readings are cheerfully undertaken as rationalizations for domination in the cases of marginalizing of women, discriminating against LGBTQ persons, or serving as a theological basis for slavery and colonialism, it is quite spectacular how non-literally Jesus's words about wealth are interpreted. As we shall see, Jesus goes to great length (especially in Luke's Gospel) to navigate the tensions of wealth and salvation history. Setting those aside for the moment, we turn to examine his warnings about the dangers of wealth, and the centrality of the *ptoxoi* to his ministry.

To bolster the roots of ptoxocracy within the Christian tradition, we turn to evidence of the centrality of the *ptoxoi* in Jesus's ministry. A few other New Testament citations also demonstrate the ways that Jesus's own followers understood the centrality of the poor to his mission. A full

12. Coffin, *Passion for the Possible*, 62–68.

accounting of Jesus's use of the word *ptoxoi* in the four Gospels could fill the pages of an entire book, but a summary can give us an appreciation of the depth of Jesus's concern and thinking about the *ptoxoi*—that is, the materially poor—as we embark in this direction.

A favorite passage of stewardship homilies, Mark 12 tells the story of Jesus watching people at the temple in Jerusalem give money and his commentary. Rich (*plusioi*) persons come forward and give large sums, likely garnering deep cries of appreciation from the glowing crowds. When a poor (*ptoxoi*) widow comes forward and delivers two copper coins, Jesus commends her, "for all of *them*"—that is, the *plusioi*—"have contributed out of their abundance, but she out of her poverty has put in everything she had, all she had to live on" (Mark 12:44; italics mine). This passage shows an implicit condemnation of the rich and favor of the poor. In fact, the next words from Jesus's mouth in Mark are a condemnation of the circumstances of temple culture—that is, a social and religious structure that would give rise and allow for such mistreatment of the poor. Luke's account of this same scene contrasts the true gift of the woman's two copper pennies to the "beautiful stones" of the temple with even greater clarity. "As for these things that you see," says Jesus, speaking of the temple, "as for these things that you see, the days will come when not one stone will be left upon another; all will be thrown down" (Luke 21:6). It is this very threat, a threat uttered against a system of wealth that seeks no interest in the poor, that will be used as evidence to condemn Jesus when he stands before both Pilate and the Sanhedrin.

During his ministry Jesus would speak parable after parable, teaching after teaching that have to do with the *ptoxoi*. In Luke's Gospel, Jesus encourages listeners to consider inviting the *ptoxoi* to feasts: "But when you give a banquet," he says, "invite the poor, the crippled, the lame, and the blind" (Luke 14:13). Zacchaeus encounters a pronouncement of salvation from Jesus when he declares his intention to give half his possessions and anything he has defrauded to the *ptoxoi* (Luke 19:8). In Matthew's Gospel a man asks how he might receive eternal life, only to have Jesus ask him to recite some basic commandments. When the man claims he has fulfilled all of these, Jesus responds, "If you wish to be perfect, go, sell your possessions, and give the money to the poor, and you will have treasure in heaven; then come, follow me" (Matt 19:21). Whether or not we are supposed to take Jesus's command to sell our possessions literally is one question, but hardly in question is the idea that followers of Jesus ought to have concern for, and even a stake in, the lives of the poor. To whatever degree Jesus intends his followers to give up their own wealth, it is clear that the lives of the poor and the central priorities of Christian faith are intimately intertwined.

Jesus warns of the dangers of wealth with such frequency that it's a wonder a rich person would show their face in Christian community at all. In Matt 6, Jesus reminds listeners that one cannot serve wealth and God. The rich wonder, later in the same Gospel, when they had seen (and ignored) the poor during their earthly lives. Jesus responds in concluding this eschatological description of end-times reckoning that would make any serious listener's hair stand on end: "Truly I tell you, just as you did it to one of the least of these brothers and sisters of mine"—that is, the *ptoxoi*—"you did to me" (Matt 25:40b). Yet it wasn't as if Jesus hadn't given us a warning on his way to this moment: "Then Jesus said to his disciples, 'Truly I tell you, it will be hard for a rich person to enter the kingdom of heaven. Again I tell you, it is easier for a camel to go through the eye of a needle than for someone who is rich to enter the kingdom of God'" (Matt 19:23–24). Or when, in Mark's Gospel, Jesus tells a parable of a weed choking out the seeds of God's word, "And others are those sown among the thorns: these are the ones who hear the word, but the cares of the age and the lure of wealth and the desire for other things come in and choke the word, and it yields nothing" (Mark 4:18–19).

The point of this examination is not to take literal account of Jesus's words and actions, but to demonstrate the centrality of the *ptoxoi* to his ministry. The poor are not an afterthought in Jesus's teaching; rather, they are central to its design, content, mission, and expression. Jesus is not accidental about the ways he understands economic realities as a central concern to human flourishing. "For you always have the poor"—that is, the *ptoxoi*—"with you, but you will not always have me," Jesus says (Matt 26:11). On the one hand, we might be tempted to hear Jesus as admitting defeat, as in: whatever you try to accomplish, you'll still be stuck with poor people. However, there's another way to read this: the blessing of God to the *ptoxoi*, whom the world chooses to curse and forget, will always be available to them in the present time. God's blessing to the poor is not a once and done thing—it is a counteractive measure, a condition that is realized with each curse, each time the word *ptoxoi* is spat out in the mouths of the wealthy.

The apostle James, early leader of the Jesus-following community in Jerusalem, could see the disastrous relationship between the rich and poor.

"But you," he writes, following his reassertion of Jesus's proclamation that the poor will inherit the kingdom of God, "have dishonored the poor person. Is it not the rich who oppress you? Is it not they who drag you into the courts? Is it not they who blaspheme the excellent name that was invoked over you?" (Jas 2:6–7). Jesus's life among the poor, as well as the authentic witness of those closest to him, demonstrates that we ought to take Jesus's concern for the *ptoxoi* (as well as our nervousness about rich rulers) more seriously.

THE PLUSIOI, THE PTOXOI, AND THE KINGDOM OF GOD

The story becomes more complex, however, when we note that the tensions of wealth and poverty, while they extend to the ptoxocratic project inherent in Jesus's earthly ministry, do not extend to acts of God's salvation. Jesus navigates these tensions in ways that can serve as models for preachers today, and for faithful rich people who might be tempted toward hopelessness in the face of ptoxocratic authority.

The Lukan telling of the story of two restored daughters at the end of the eighth chapter serves to highlight the tense complexity of relationships that govern and define the boundaries of those who possess privilege and those who do not. The story of these two daughters—one, a twelve-year-old daughter of a synagogue leader named Jairus, and one an unnamed woman hemorrhaging blood for twelve years—demonstrates the ways that those without power are forced to navigate in a world that refuses recognition of their dignity. It demonstrates what is true for Jesus, both throughout the Gospel stories, as well for salvation history to come—namely, that although the *ptoxoi* remain central to the mission of the nearness of the dominion of God, this centrality does not come at the expense of God's love for the rich. In other words, just because God actively chooses a preferential option for the poor and authorizes the poor alone for governance, this does not mean that the rich are excluded from the love of God. The good news of God's grace extends to all, including the rich. While it extends to the rich and poor alike, extension of love does not authorize domination in any direction.

In the eighth chapter of Luke's Gospel we meet Jairus, a man who is used to handling himself in front of people of power. Not unlike the centurion in Luke's earlier story who boldly sends messengers to Jesus to heal a favored servant, Jairus is unafraid to approach Jesus with his request directly. The centurion's words in chapter 7 could easily be found in Jairus's mouth as a leader of the local synagogue. "Speak the word, and let my servant be healed," he says, "for I also am a man set under authority, with soldiers under me; and I say to one, 'Go,' and he goes, and to another, 'Come,' and he comes, and to my slave, 'Do this,' and the slave does it" (Luke 7:7b–8). Like the centurion, Jairus approaches Jesus directly with a request that the healer might deploy his power on behalf of someone he loves. Contrasting Jairus and the centurion, however, "the woman [with a flow of blood] approaches Jesus from behind, unlike Jairus, who falls at Jesus' feet."[13] The approaches to Jesus, and the significance of those approaches, could not be more different. Jairus, someone used to dealing in the world of power and privilege, requests Jesus's healing power straightforwardly. The nameless woman, by contrast, approaches Jesus from behind and in secret. She touches the hem of his garment, reaching out in desperation and faith, an approach to Jesus's healing power that could not be more opposite to the centurion and Jairus. This difference in the assumptions of privilege could not be more striking.

Without employing the Greek *ptoxoi* in this case, Luke adds a detail that colors the conversation further. The woman with a hemorrhage for twelve years "had spent all she had on physicians" (8:43b). This one detail, so inconspicuous yet devastating, tells us that she belongs among the *ptoxoi* because of her physical ailment. In other words, her economic reality as a poor person is completely tied to a physical problem. She has spent every cent she had on treatments and nothing has helped. A small detail that might be easy to miss, this economic and bodily connection is one that the poor of our present context might recognize altogether too well. Researchers in 2019, seeking data on whether the Affordable Care Act had reduced the enormous medical debt load of Americans, found that a whopping 65.5 percent of respondents who had declared bankruptcy that year had done so as a direct result of medical debt.[14] This is an outstanding figure, and one that poor people in the United States understand as deeply as did the nameless woman with a flow of blood. Debt, poverty, illness, and a burdensome system of healthcare management that favors profits over health, reduce the poor to nameless bankruptcy. The connection between bodily ailment and economic status reminds us that often the *ptoxoi* of the world exist not because of any lack of skill or desire, but because the systems of the world do not account for their well-being. That is to say, the systems of the world have no meaningful stake in their well-being. So, responding to this reality,

13. Levine and Witherington, *Gospel of Luke*, 241.
14. Himmelstein et al., "Medical Bankruptcy."

the poor woman approaches Jesus in secret, and from behind, while Jairus does so openly.

There are several implications of this story and its relationship to ptoxocracy. First, the story is clear to highlight the ways that people belonging to different social locations are conscious of approaching the divine. It demonstrates the ways that, despite Jesus's explicit naming of the *ptoxoi* as central to the expression of his gospel mission (Luke 4), social realities can continue to keep the *ptoxoi* at a distance, confined to an expression of faithfulness that falls outside socially accepted norms. It also reveals the ways that the bodily and economic realities of poor and marginalized persons can create barriers to religious practice or expression. Economic realities, in other words, affect the ways and modes that major swaths of people can approach faithful communities, and by extension, encounter faithful witness to the healing love of Jesus. As a woman with a flow of blood, this daughter's ritual impurity would both render her an outsider in the Jewish community context, and unable to enter the temple.[15] She is both poor and impure, an outsider if there ever was one.

Yet there is another implication of this story that bears theological fruit for our ptoxocratic argument: in the economy of God's healing love as revealed and witnessed in the story of Jesus through the Lukan text, Jesus meets both the rich and the poor exactly where they are, no matter what means of approach they employ. Jesus displays not only a magnanimous sense of attention to Jairus's daughter's ailment upon request, but also to the nameless woman with a flow of blood. On the one hand, this tells us that the grace of God is not confined to the rich who understand the procedures and practices of social norms (i.e., how to approach a revered healer), but to the poor as well who might not. However, it should also be noted that with the appearance of the *ptoxoi* at his feet, having approached from a social location of shame and vulnerability (behind), while Jesus displays a careful attention to her concerns during that moment, Jesus also does not abandon Jairus's daughter. The preferential option chooses attention to the woman at his feet, but it does not abandon a dying little girl, no matter her economic reality. It moves in both directions without expense of either. Salvation is as much a reality for the rich daughter as well as the poor one. This is in stark contrast to the medical-industrial complex of the United States, a system which bankrupts families with burdensome debts to treat chronic health issues. In other words, attention to the needs of the poor never comes at

---

15. Levine and Witherington, *Gospel of Luke*, 241.

the salvific expense of the rich within the dominion of God. Luke's story of the two daughters gives us a glimpse of the radical way in which the love of God exists for both rich and poor and invites us to imagine human systems that do likewise.

This is hardly the first or last time in Luke's Gospel that readers are invited into the tension of Jesus's complex relationship between rich and poor. As Amy-Jill Levine and Ben Witherington III point out, though Jesus explicitly names good news to the poor as a priority of his earthly mission, he hardly demands that his followers create a movement (a church) of the poor at the full exclusion of the rich. Starting with some of the disciples, Luke's Gospel proceeds to give salvific concern to a parade of characters we would not classify as *ptoxoi*, Jairus's daughter being one of many. These include four disciples who own boats, Zacchaeus the chief tax collector, the centurion and his sick servant, Levi the tax collector, homeowners Martha and Mary, the host of seemingly wealthy women named in chapter 7 who minister to the disciples, and various Pharisees he meets along the way.[16] Moreover, when John the Baptist was out near the Jordan dunking folks in the river, many of these same sorts of figures came his way asking for advice. Rather than outrightly condemning the reality of their station or wealth, he responds with advice that acknowledges the temptations that their positions imply (tax collecting and soldiering), and encourage moderate faithfulness and honesty as the best course of action (Luke 3:12–14).

All this is to say that, as in the system of ptoxocracy, there is a place in the kingdom of God for persons of wealth, and that the nearness of the kingdom of God does not despise or reject these out of hand. Rather, Luke's Gospel, which begins by acknowledging a wealthy patron named Theophilus (Luke 1:1–4), understands Jesus's mission to be radical insofar as it refuses the logic of domination, a logic which sets classes of persons against one another, a logic that undermines the potential for consensus and moderation. Luke's Jesus is clear, however, that the only way of building this kind of earthly middle way is through an explicit blessing of the poor as those deemed capable and worthy of ruling authority. Jesus's stake in the poor, therefore, nourishes the whole community.

Finally, Jesus follows the logic of his Jewish forebears in understanding the relationship between rich and poor, and preserving God's preferential option for the poor. In other words, he didn't invent it. "In the Jewish tradition," write Levine and Witherington, "disabled individuals together with

---

16. Levine and Witherington, *Gospel of Luke*, 177.

the poor, the widow, the orphan, and the stranger are under God's special protection . . . because they are more socially vulnerable."[17] Jesus's mother Mary, echoing the song of Hannah before her in the book of 1 Samuel, sings of exactly this sort of divine priority when he is still in her womb. As some have noted, much of Jesus's earthly teaching seems to be the embodiment of Mary's song to such an extent that we can appreciate that he learned this theology from her. As Howard Thurman writes, "It is impossible for Jesus to be understood outside of the sense of community which Israel held with God. . . . Here is one who was so conditioned and organized within himself that he became a perfect instrument for the embodiment of a set of ideals."[18] This is important because it not only pushes against an ugly history of Christian anti-Semitism, but because it roots ptoxocracy within the rich tradition of Hebrew prophets whose articulation of God's concern for the poor predates Jesus.

These prophets of the Hebrew Bible spoke at long length to the connection between the exploitation of the poor at the hands of the rich. The prophet Amos explicitly connects the unheeded cries of the poor to God's anger and justice. The rich continue to worship God as if their personal devotion and sacrifice ought to be enough, forgetting that God's truest desire is not worship, but love of neighbor. "I hate, I despise your festivals," says God, "and I take no delight in your solemn assemblies. Even though you offer me your burnt offerings and grain offerings, I will not accept them, and the offerings of well-being of your fatted animals I will not look upon" (Amos 5:21–22). The most famous and beautiful passage that follows is directed squarely at the rich, highlighting the centrality of the poor: "But let justice roll down like water and righteousness like an ever-flowing stream" (5:24). God will not abide the sounds of the rich as they feast and offer up goods in divine praise while they trample the frail and weak. God will not be bought off to authorize their domination. Amos connects the plight of the poor to the actions of the rich that God finds expressly abhorrent. They plant and harvest at the expense of the poor, not to their benefit, and this systematic mistreatment of the poor rouses divine anger precisely because God holds a stake in the lives of the poor.

The middle way between rich and poor is charted as a course by Jesus in his parables. While multiple parables in Luke's Gospel may be helpful in articulating a ptoxocratic relationship between rich and poor, one stands

---

17. Levine and Witherington, *Gospel of Luke*, 145.
18. Thurman, *Jesus and the Disinherited*, 5–6.

over the rest. Sitting at the table among rich and poor alike in the home of a Pharisee, Jesus invites his followers to notice the ways that the power of wealth translates into the power of ruling. "When you are invited by someone to a wedding banquet, do not sit down at the place of honor, in case someone more distinguished than you has been invited by your host, and the host who invited both of you may come and say to you, 'Give this person your place,' and then in disgrace you would start to take the lowest place" (Luke 14:8–9). The ways we elevate certain persons over others due to financial status are clearly at work here, and Jesus invites his disciples to see the world differently. He continues, "When you give a luncheon or a dinner, do not invite your friends or your brothers and sisters or your relatives or rich neighbors, in case they may invite you in return, and you would be repaid. But when you give a banquet, invite the poor, the crippled, the lame, and the blind. And you will be blessed because they cannot repay you, for you will be repaid at the resurrection of the righteous (Luke 14:13–14). Clearly articulating the relationship of rich and poor as tense in the best of times, Jesus invites the rich into a salvific relinquishing of the opportunity to translate wealth into political power. The rich have little to gain in inviting the poor to parties, which is exactly the point.

Nothing in these parables lends credibility to the idea that the rich possess any divine right of domination or ruling authority. Quite the opposite, in fact. Amos, like Jesus, reminds us of the perpetual temptations of the rich toward myopia, how easily the poor are forgotten when the bellies of the rich are full. Acknowledging the tension in this relationship, Jesus paves a middle way that is ptoxocratic in nature. By authorizing the poor for ruling power, he relieves the rich of the opportunity of actions that are damaging to the soul. Yet, this relief does not mean that Jesus forgets or hates the wealthy. As the story of Jairus and the two daughters reminds us, Jesus is perfectly capable of extending salvation in both directions, at the expense of neither party.

This is an important point for followers of Jesus in the twenty-first century in the Global North, and one that resonates deeply with me out of pastoral concern. There is ever a tension in the pulpit between the words of Jesus and the faces of the assembly before you, most of whom are counted among the rich. It is important to acknowledge the maintenance of good news for the rich despite Jesus's ptoxocratic tendencies, which are often heard as bad news in the ears of rich listeners because they encourage the emptying out of one's of power. My concern here, I suppose, is born of experience. The most faithful expression of parish ministry I can articulate is one that recognizes the contributions of Gutiérrez and liberation theologians to the contemporary challenges of our time. Yet in teaching or preaching these, one smacks against the reality of wealthy persons in the assembly. My point here is that Jesus understood this tension well, and that modeling our lives and ministries after Jesus's means both examining mythologies of the rich ruling class (as Jesus does in the parable above), explicitly naming the salvific reality of God's love for all economic classes of people, all the while authorizing the poor for ruling authority via ptoxocratic inferences in his teaching. Rather than avoid this tension altogether, an avoidance that will likely come at the expense of the poor, we are invited to wade into the discomfort. It's a tough course to navigate, yet if Jesus can find a way to set a common table among sex workers, fishermen, and rich tax collectors all at once, so can we.

CONCLUSION

The roots of ptoxocracy dangle into the very scriptural soils where human rulers have sought to plant their authority for generations. Not only does scriptural witness undermine claims of domination by the rich, but it expressly opposes it and authorizes the poor as rulers. Given the history of Western political discourse and its constant reversion to Christian Scripture as a source of authority, the political implications of this argument from theology are significant. The worrisome relationship between Christian doctrine and despots has been long documented, and it's important that the very documents cited as evidence for domination of the poor should be used as their undoing. Any structure or government that finds authority for oppression of the poor from within the Christian tradition is either willfully blind or flagrantly misleading. In the final analysis, ptoxocratic assertions and forms emerge from out of the Gospels, and from the very heart of the Christian tradition. As such, it is from the practitioners of that very tradition from which they could most easily flow. It is this idea toward which we now turn our imaginations.

6

Ptoxocracy and the Church

Gracious Father, we pray for your holy catholic church. Fill it with all truth and peace. Where it is corrupt, purify it; where it is in error, direct it; where in anything it is amiss, reform it; where it is right, strengthen it; where it is in need, provide for it; where it is divided, reunite it.[1]

IT IS AN ADMITTEDLY GARGANTUAN expectation of modern politics to believe that ptoxocracy might be able to wade through the distortion of power and wealth and into its purest expression without guidance. I have until now merely hoped to provide a possible (if small) theoretical, philosophical, and theological pathway toward structurally instituting a meaningful stake in the lives of the poor in civil society. Whether possibility translates into actuality is for history to decide.

But because I am a pastor of a church in North America, it is time that I brought the argument closer to home. As I compose this book, my denomination, the Evangelical Lutheran Church in America (ELCA), is in a multi-year visioning process called "Commission for a Renewed Lutheran Church." The commission seems to have arisen out of the urgency of both a decline in membership and an acknowledgment of institutional deficiency, especially regarding the acknowledgment of structural racism. The anxiety is that this decline in participation and membership in North American churches is a deadly one, sapping the church at large of precious resources,

---

1. Evangelical Lutheran Church in America, *Evangelical Lutheran Worship*, 58.

but also of hope. More urgently, however, is the reality that the ELCA continues to be one of the least diverse bodies of mainline denominational North American Christianity. Somehow, after more than thirty years of life as the nation's second largest Protestant denomination and countless efforts and dollars spent to diversify the ELCA, we are more staunchly a white church than ever. Something seems to be wrong, and the commission's job is to analyze the structures and governance in place that might be barriers to this denominational phenomenon. More than thirty persons, ranging from pastors and theologians to systems experts and lay leaders are directly engaged in this process. Whether we might be optimistic that these leaders will produce a church that is altered much from its most destructive human tendencies has yet to be seen and is outside the scope of this book's analysis.

Lest I commit the sin of pointing out structural problems in civic governance without addressing my own organization's shortcomings—one thinks here of Jesus's saying on pointing out the speck in a neighbor's eye while refusing to deal with the plank in my own (Matt 7:3)—I want to suggest that ptoxocracy might provide a novel structural solution to the ills of my, or any other, Christian structure or denomination. By electing to institute a ptoxocratic mechanism into the constituting documents of each congregation, as well as its synodical (local/regional) and church-wide (national or global) expressions, the ELCA might begin to address its own barriers to diversity by way of its own meaningful investment in the lives of the poor. In the words of Greg Boyle, "God stands with the powerless not to console them in their powerlessness, but to always remind them of their power. Hence, Jesus critiques all forms of domination and we are compelled to do the same as Church."[2] If concern for the *ptoxoi* was as central to Jesus's ministry as I have argued, it follows that ptoxocracy is one possible mechanism that the church might employ in waging this critique.

As I begin to explore such planks in our collective eyes as the church, I must note that such a critique is done in a loving spirit, rather than a harmful one. I am reminded of one prayer option for Reformation Sunday that serves as this chapter's epigraph. It is my genuine belief that any expression of church, my own denomination included, contains a mixture of both the deeply flawed and the deeply good.

---

2. Boyle, *Whole Language*, 135.

ORGANIZING THE CHURCH

To begin, it's helpful to analyze the system of constituted order as we find it. Suffice it to say that the constituted order of the church—that is, the way that it chooses to orient itself by way of elected officers and members as an institution—mirrors American democratic principles. As one church leadership expert, Dan Hotchkiss, writes, "Civil government and congregations have exerted mutual influence in North America since colonial times."[3] Like the US, congregations elect representatives who do the more detailed day-to-day work of enacting policies and supporting paid staff. We find a church who elects officers and board members from out of an assembly much like the representational democratic system of American government. When examining the organization from a structural perspective, we find many of the same hallmarks of organizational principles as we find within representative democracy, with judiciary capacities, a legislative body with capacity to enact policy and set budgets, as well as a small executive cohort to handle both in-depth and confidential matters on behalf of the congregation at large. As Hotchkiss puts it, "In the U.S. national tradition 'we the people' exercise our sovereignty through representatives, and Americans tend to assume congregations should be organized that way as well."[4] Whether the reader belongs to a Protestant denomination in the United States or not, it is further the case that the church is not alone among nonprofits in governing itself this way.

Returning to Jesus's Sermons, both on the Plain and the Mount, however, it's hard to imagine that Jesus would have imagined a future body of his followers constituting themselves as such. In the introduction to this book, I noted the work of historian Anthony Kaldellis, who remarks that there is more of Roman structure in church organization than not, and that this would likely baffle early Christians, whose early antagonisms at the hands of Rome led to existential consequence. With Kaldellis, we can wonder what kind of organizational structure the early church had imagined, though we can look to Scripture to supply some hints. The earliest body of Jesus followers, according to the book of Acts, transformed their individual possessions into a collective purse, implying a structure that outrightly abolished private property: "All who believed were together and had all things in common; they would sell their possessions and goods

---

3. Hotchkiss, *Governance and Ministry*, 67.
4. Hotchkiss, *Governance and Ministry*, 67.

and distribute the proceeds to all, as any had need" (Acts 2:44–45). These simple verses have led many at the intersection of political philosophy and theology to wonder whether the organizational structure might look more like what modern readers understand as anarcho-communist in form. We, however, having examined Jesus's authorization of the poor as rulers, can see that these forms may also more faithfully take on the structural suggestions of ptoxocracy. Regardless, it does not take much poking around Scripture to find a disconnect between the church as we find it, and the form scriptural witnesses had imagined it might become.

The options for the church in countering the empire's grasp two thousand years later are many. The faithful, for example, might completely detach themselves from the state and seek to form a new society based exclusively on the Gospels. One can look to the vast movements of monastics and aesthetics on the one hand, or varied Anabaptist communities within North America to see what a rejection of civil society as we know it might look like. Whether one agrees with the moral choices of these groups, one must admire their tenacity to hold fast to the words of Jesus in the face of the ceaseless powers and pressures from capitalism and the US government through time. Yet it is hard to see whether this expression, detached from engagement with outside communities as some of them are, are native to faith in Jesus. Since Jesus went beyond the bounds of his own community into gentile (literally, the nations) territory, it is hard to see how communal governing systems native to Christianity would be purely inward-facing in form.

Another option is to cede the lost ground to Rome and turn one's attention to other meaningful ways of engaging Jesus's teaching. I would argue that this has been the tactic of my tradition, as it is most of North America's mainline denominations, in seeking to accept the system as we have inherited it today and to attempt to peaceably work within it. This is a tactic of poking and prodding at it from the present moral perspective as followers of Jesus without totally dismissing such structures. One must admit, however, the dissatisfaction and contradictions one must endure day after day in this option. To live in empire is to become complicit in the crimes it perpetuates, especially those perpetual sins against the poor and marginalized. To live blindly within the empire is constantly to turn one's back on fundamental aspects of Jesus's teaching, and to become complicit in its dealings, especially regarding the poor. While I am grateful to be a pastor within a denomination that attempts to navigate this tension consciously, I feel the pressures of this decision from within and without, as a teacher, preacher, and leader. There are absolutely ways in which those inward-facing communities have more faithfully adhered to Jesus's vision than have our empire-complicit communities.

Returning to the story of Jairus's daughter and the woman with the flow of blood explored in the previous chapter helps to frame the issue here. The challenge is to imagine a possibility in which we can embody Jesus's ministry to both Jairus's daughter and the daughter with the flow of blood whom Jesus heals. Jesus attends to both, and so should we. In the fractured reality of Christianity today each body must decide for itself how to navigate these polarities in structure, though our present course of attending to Jairus's needs over the nameless daughter's is troubling. We attend to Jairus's daughter structurally, and to the nameless daughter with a flow of blood by charity. These are not equal forms of attention. For example, while leaders serving on church boards are reimbursed for travel expenses, they are not generally compensated for their time, which means that most church decision-makers are from among the class of persons who can afford to volunteer. Jairus often has a seat at a structural decision-making table, but the nameless woman does not. He is looked upon as a helper, and she as a problem to be solved. This is a dynamic we will explore more thoroughly in the next chapter through the lens of ptoxocracy. Examples like this demonstrate the ways that Christian systems of governance hold a structurally meaningful stake in the lives of the rich, and a weaker, more optional, stake in the lives of the poor.

Given these current realities for North American Lutherans, my hope is to articulate one possible vision for a renewed ELCA through our present analysis of ptoxocracy. The vision is at once both very simple and extremely radical: the injection of a requirement that the only persons eligible for election to democratic representation within church government are the *ptoxoi*, the materially poor. If one takes the argument of ptoxocracy seriously, as well as its roots within the preaching of Jesus and theological traditions therein, it follows that ptoxocracy is a faithful response to church structure. Since we have already examined ptoxocracy as a modification of representative democracy, and since denominations largely contain many of the structural contours of secular representative democracies, the leap to ptoxocracy is a relatively small one. Because congregations often function in such representative models, the centers of ruling authority rest within governing boards (or in the ELCA's case, church councils), so the injection of ptoxocracy might be made exactly at this point, with the only members of the body eligible for election to these boards drawn from among the *ptoxoi*.

Since we can largely imagine the contours of this decision based on the previous chapters, the exploration of this chapter will deal specifically with its implications for church structure. Overall, such a ptoxocratic change to the constitutional order of congregations and church structures would have three major implications. First, it would realize the Christian tradition's hope of existing for the sake of the world (echoing Jesus's words), and moreover its recentering on the needs of the poor. It would likely yield a church that less resembles the prefect of Rome than the church of Saint Lawrence, something I believe it understands intuitively though struggles to articulate. Next, it would transform the church into a mechanism by which poor persons attain actual power within communities, even those beyond the congregation itself. Finally, it would transform the ways that the church is perceived outside its walls, yielding a church that is perceived as more authentic to its neighbors.

A CHURCH FOR THE PTOXOI

The simple ptoxocratic alteration of constitutional order by way of eligibility requirement would undercut some of the implicit disdain for poor persons within the order as it stands today, at least within a local parish community. For example, it is generally taken to be good practice of congregations to elect persons to positions of board leadership who are identified as having a strong stake in the outcome of the church. This mirrors the practice of most healthy nonprofits and is taken to be among best practices of leadership. Experts like Dan Hotchkiss—whose work, I should note, has been massively helpful in my own pastoral leadership—suggest that the best orientation of board leadership is that they conceive of themselves as stakeholders in the entity, that they work for the mission of the church.[5] Hotchkiss rejects the idea of board members as mere representatives of the will of the people, and promotes the idea of stakeholders as more effective and helpful. I agree wholeheartedly. I have sat on many church councils whose members believe themselves to represent some undefined will of the congregation, and these tend to be ineffective at best. That's not how representative democracy is designed to function in secular government, nor

---

5. Hotchkiss, *Governance and Ministry*, 70.

should it be how congregational board members conceive of themselves. It is far more effective to identify key stakeholders in the mission and vision of the organization.

Yet this raises the question: who, then, is in the best position to be identified as stakeholders? What conditions make for great board leaders as stakeholders? As in actual holding of a stake, those who are able to purchase stock. Those who are known to have invested the most capital in the outcome of the project. Following Hotchkiss, those who donate money to fund the nonprofit's work are an easy place to start. Most churches would take these to be the highest givers. Now, before feeling altogether cynical about this idea, consider that those who donate large sums to churches are not always the richest people. In a voluntary organization the opposite is often true. Sometimes generosity and wealth are not true correlates. As a pastor in an actual church, I do tend to subscribe to the idea that stakeholding, especially as measured in actual donations, can be a powerful criterion for identifying those volunteers who might do well in positions of church leadership. It helps me identify who has actual skin in the game, and who is just along for the ride. In the words of church fundraising specialist J. Clif Christopher, "Giving is the closest thing we have on a daily basis to getting a true picture of a person's character."[6] Because donating money is an external indication, it can be one of the only metrics churches have in gauging stakeholder interest, in fact. Yet, what can also happen, especially in Protestant churches whose donations are confidential even to the pastor and nominating committee, is that the perceived largest donors are identified and selected as board members. Following Christopher's advice that pastors know the giving of their members, I am constantly astounded by this at nearly every church where I have served. Because this is sensitive information, and because I am one of the only persons in the church who knows donation amounts, I understand the ways that wealth can entitle some to a presumption of generosity, how those who are known to be most wealthy are assumed to be the most generous. (Usually, the loudest are also perceived to be the most generous also, though that has yet to be proven correct in any church setting I've known.) Fascinatingly, it is seldom the wealthiest in a congregation who give in highest proportion to their income, as both Christopher and Hotchkiss also note. Rather, it is usually those with less who tend to give more. I've found that while donations can be a pretty good indicator of commitment and passion, I've also learned

6. Christopher, *Not Your Parents' Offering Plate*, chap. 8.

never to assume that the wealthiest members are the most generous, even while they are assumed to be. Jesus's commendation of the widow's mite in Luke's Gospel tells us that this may indeed be a timeless reality.

There are ways of contextualizing and nuancing this understanding, of course, which is a discussion for another time. My point here is that churches, both formally and informally, already take one's economic standing as an acceptable means of measuring commitment and eligibility for decision-making leadership. Ironically, churches tend to be culturally allergic to speaking outrightly about money, so that many of these conversations never actually take place at all. Whereas Jesus spoke about money in nearly every other Gospel passage, it seems his contemporary followers prefer to be more polite. Not only that, to overtly acknowledge economic factors as viable indicators of, say, commitment, is to break the fourth wall of pastoral and religious interaction. Yet wealth and economic status do matter in church politics, much as we prefer to believe they do not: those church members who demonstrate that professional success yields wealth are likeliest to be tapped as decision-makers and potential board members. This likely varies with each context. Wealth yields decision-making power, even in church governance.

Another place that pastors and church leaders tend to see this is when it comes time to negotiate a pastor's salary, where the pastor is an assumed stakeholder in the values of faith (which is not a bad assumption), and expected to consciously navigate the dynamics of power and wealth with intention. By way of anecdote, which is shaky evidence at best but helps to contextualize my ideas for nonchurch leaders, a friend of mine recently took an opportunity to interview for a pastoral position in a predominantly white wealthy suburban church. She was honored to be called to one of the denomination's most prestigious communities of faith in that region, a church that was known to be well-endowed and well-heeled. Yet, surrounded by board members, many of whom worked in the corporate landscape of the city, she felt totally unseen and hurt when it came time to negotiate her salary. The salary they handed to her was so low, so absurdly out of touch with costs of living in that neighborhood, that she laughed audibly when she received it. The people in the room were aghast when their possible future pastor balked. In speaking to the president of the council privately afterward, she discovered that it wasn't so low because the church didn't have money, but because the church didn't feel it was culturally acceptable to pay a pastor the wage that might have made it possible for her to live in the community she intended to serve. It was an expensive neighborhood, and they felt it was culturally inappropriate to offer a disciple of Jesus so much for her labor. In other words, they understood a call to ministry as a call to poverty, just like Jesus. The pastor replied that as followers of Jesus themselves, might the board members themselves see the need to follow his example of poverty in their own lives. This, she reported, now made the council president laugh.

This is anecdotal evidence to be sure, but the story shows that sensitivity to poverty is not foreign to board leadership, and neither is sensitivity to personal economics. Protestants in America understand Jesus's call to serve the poor in some senses, by way of showing up at food banks and shelters, donating money to causes, living generously, expecting their pastors to live modestly, and so on. I have no doubt that the members of my church understand, if only vaguely, the importance of wealth and money as it bears down on the moral fabric of the human soul. But at the end of the day, once again, the Roman Empire speaks more loudly than does Jesus on this issue. In assuming that the theological commitment to the poor only extends to or obliges pastoral leaders to lives of poverty, board members essentially export aspects of their faith that are inconvenient. Such is the condition of human sin that it forgets attending to the one with the flow of blood may also mean empowering her as a structural decision-making force within the community so that the community may cast a wider net for stakes in the lives of those within their midst.

Once a man asked Jesus what he must do inherit eternal life. He kept the commandments, gave charity to the poor, and seemed to be genuinely interested. Jesus suggested he rid himself of all his possessions and give the money to the poor. The man walked away in despair, for, as the Gospel writer tells us, "He had many possessions" (Luke 6:20–21). Again, we understand perfectly well that following Jesus has something to do with mindfulness about money, we just don't seem interested in pointing judgment in our own direction when acknowledging it. That challenge is for the pastor to undertake, or the radical ascetic, but not us. In other words, churches are good at compartmentalizing the commands of Jesus, attributing some to one segment of their population, while ignoring it for another. There's nothing special about this. As a Lutheran theologian I am committed to a particularly cosmic and all-encompassing idea of sin, one which more than accounts for the ways that even church organizations can be so myopic about their own theological commitments.

By inserting a ptoxocratic criteria into the governing documents of churches, however, the church would explicitly recognize the importance of economic standing as a fundamental facet to one's capacity to serve as an institutional stakeholder. If God holds a stake in the lives of the *ptoxoi*, then the *ptoxoi* are the true stakeholders of the church.

GIFT ECONOMIES

In the previous chapter we explored the roots of ptoxocracy within Christian theology, and most especially within the New Testament. Yet even as Christian theology has potential to imagine new economies of power within the heart of its sacred texts, there are other good-faith partners doing exactly this kind of work already, and we do not have to reject the given structures of empire alone. We'll explore some of these in the next chapter. One of these is from writer and scientist Robin Wall Kimmerer, whose *The Serviceberry* explores alternative structures of mutual flourishing between creatures. Kimmerer, a botanist by trade, examines the sources of what she calls the *gift economy* from both her perspective as an enrolled member of the Citizen Potawatomi Nation, and as an observer of the kinds of economies that exists between living plants in the field of botany. She writes that "gratitude and reciprocity are the currency of a gift economy,"[7] ideas of a structure that could just as easily emerge from out of the Christian tradition. Kimmerer, steeped in an examination of the ecological devastation wrought at the hands of industrial economies, begins her work by asking, "When an economic system actively destroys what we love, isn't it time for a new system?"[8] The question could just as easily arise from out of the heart of the Christian story, a story that insists that the death-dealing forces of the Roman empire so perfectly typified in the cruelty of crucifixion, cannot ultimately triumph over the resurrective life of God. One sees the supreme irony of Christian history in conforming to Roman structures of economics, politics, and governance, structures that diminish rather than center the priorities of Jesus—that is, the well-being of all persons in society including the *ptoxoi*.

Kimmerer writes, "The currency in a gift economy is relationship, which is expressed as gratitude, as interdependence, and the ongoing cycles of reciprocity. A gift economy nurtures the community bonds that enhance

---

7. Kimmerer, *Serviceberry*, 14.
8. Kimmerer, *Serviceberry*, 18.

mutual well-being. The economic unit is 'we' rather than 'I,' as all flourishing is mutual."[9] I suspect that many other pastors know what I know, which is that despite our conformity to the empire's systems, we, the church, already know how to do this. Recently I took on the responsibility of cosupervising an intern pastor for another small congregation in my area. The man arrived in east San Diego County with an assignment from my wider church body to explore the feasibility of a new Lutheran church serving Arabic-speaking Christians whose existing theological commitments match well with those of the Lutheran tradition. He arrived, however, with very little by way of furniture, home goods, or those things that an everyday citizen of this community might take for granted. As such, my congregation, in partnership with two other local Lutheran congregations, took up the task of collecting goods to furnish his apartment. While my cosupervisor and I wrung our hands in worry that we could never find enough goods to make his home comfortable, the voice of what Kimmerer calls the scarcity economy itching in our minds, our three congregations gathered an outpouring of goods that could have furnished ten apartments. It was not the first time I had seen this happen, as my church regularly furnishes an apartment for a local program for victims of domestic violence, yet it surprised me (as it always does) nevertheless. I recognized something in this experience: I am so trained to see scarcity as the basis for our social exchange that witnessing the bounty of human generosity came as a shock, even within the church.

Christians are trained to understand acts like these as functions of charity, yet they reveal something different entirely. These congregations were not responding to the need to provide goods for this man out of moral duty to charity, but as a possibility for participation in the now-ness of the kingdom of God (as we explored in chapter 5). Such participation is, in fact, the opposite of charity, because it understands abundance, not scarcity, as the source of our being in the world. It was an experience of Kimmerer's gift economy. Such an economy, as understood by Kimmerer and others, has little use for charity for it already assumes the good of the neighbor, the good of the *ptoxoi* as a highest good. Charity, meanwhile, is necessary only within an economy that sees scarcity as its premise. It is the exception to scarcity that fuels its necessity. Witnessing my small Lutheran church respond to the needs of a person who had very little helped me realize that Christian communities already have potential for Kimmerer's gift economy, yet because we've chosen to base our structure on the economies

---

9. Kimmerer, *Serviceberry*, 33.

of scarcity, we can hardly view cases like this as anything but the exception. The Christian tradition is ripe for Kimmerer's gift economy, yet we assume that to stay vital or alive we must play by the rules of a wider society that demands scarcity, a lie that has come to define us more than we wish to admit. If Jesus was a ptoxocrat, then furnishing the apartment of a newcomer to community is not particularly novel or special, but the logical outcome of a theology that understands mutual flourishing as the highest good, a divine good.

A CHURCH AGAINST THE POOR

There exist structures of Christian community that imbue certain authorities or privileges that may or may not conform to its theological precepts. By way of another example, a retired ELCA navy chaplain once came to speak to my group of local pastors to relay the call for ELCA chaplains, asserting that chaplains from our tradition were in high demand by the armed forces and that our numbers of chaplains in the services were in decline. Part of his claim to high demand for our chaplains arose from the fact that the ELCA has more structural open communion agreements with other denominations than any other in the United States, which is to say that ELCA members and pastors may engage in sacramental practices during worship alongside members of other Christian communities without repercussion from a bishop. Couple the unique set of communion agreements with the denomination's high standards of accountability, ethical practices, and education, he invited us to begin recruitment of potential chaplains into service, as they would find easy work in the military. While this is a highly subjective claim, and one that I cannot quite substantiate with evidence, I first heard his claims and swelled with pride. That the ELCA, my denomination, might be prized among hundreds by the US government filled me with a gratitude for the many theologians, pastors, and bishops who so carefully crafted those open communion agreements, and set such high standards for ELCA pastors.

Ptoxocracy, admittedly, puts something of a damper on this source of pride. Open communion agreements that privilege the well-being and mutual flourishing of Christians over denominational squabbles are certainly well-earned sources of pride, and may even conform to ptoxocratic assertions insofar as they see mutual stakeholding as a source of good for both partners. However, a more troubling aspect of this relationship lies in the conformity of the denomination's structure to those which the armed forces recognize in legitimate partners. The ELCA's structure prizes higher education, rigorous ethical standards, and accountability—all excellent ends in-and-of-themselves. Yet the fact of their easy translation into the hierarchical power dynamics of military expectations is troubling because it highlights their conformity to the structures of violent power rather than, say, Jesus's blessing of peacemakers in the Sermon on the Mount. If it is true that some within the US military prefer ELCA chaplains (a claim which, again, is hard to verify) then one wonders how quickly a loss of this status might occur were the church to conform its structure to the kinds of ptoxocratic principles that arise out of Jesus's Sermon on the Plain.

It is not hard to imagine the ways that ptoxocracy not only pushes back but threatens the very fabric of other economies and systems of power in the world. That is exactly the point. Ptoxocracy, like Kimmerer's gift economy, yields a threatening potential to undermine the interests of powerful forces in the world. She notes that potlatches, one example of Native American expressions of the gift economy she explores, were expressly "banned by colonial governments under the influence of missionaries in the 1800s," precisely for their rejection of private property as the basis of human economies.[10] With the advantage of historical perspective, we can now see these acts clearly as destructive, violent, oppositional in nature to Christian theological claims, and oppressive. Yet as the example of furnishing the new intern's apartment shows, members of congregations know what it means to express the economy of God in just such a way. Each time my congregation supports a refugee family with goods and services, or furnishes a new home for a victim of domestic violence, these are the times when the congregation comes most alive. Yes, this liveliness also happens during ritual moments in worship, as when I lift the bread and cup, when singing together a beloved hymn, or even in moments of exchanging the peace. We witness the power and beauty of Kimmerer's gift economy each time we are invited to pour our lives out into the community by way of generosity. The structures of power as we find them today demand that such moments are the exception to the rule, that moral commitments to mutual flourishing can only be achieved through acts of charity. The point here is that the church is ever torn between participating in alternative economies of power that it understands innately, like Kimmerer's gift economy, and systems that are nonnative to its own theology, such as

---

10. Kimmerer, *Serviceberry*, 36.

US military chaplaincy. Yet the life of my congregation, as so many others would attest, is richest when we move in tandem with the kingdom of God, something we already know and understand how to do well. Ptoxocracy clarifies which of these paths arise from within the church, and those that do not.

A PTOXOCRATIC CHURCH

It seems the church is at a delicate position. We find ourselves surrounded by the vestiges of the Roman empire—that is, an economy based on private property, scarcity, and land ownership. It is a vestige that has wreaked havoc on the lives of the disenfranchised and marginalized. Meanwhile, we hold commitments according to Christian faith that betray the world we live in at nearly every step. Fascinatingly, the church, and most precisely here I mean the ELCA, is not poor. The ELCA holds endowments, properties, and associates with a network of churches across the globe with vast resources. Yet decline and stagnation are setting in, rendering those investments with fewer and fewer future inheritors. It is no wonder that a wave of reconciliation-minded folks should beg the church to invest in reconstituting herself, attempting to right the structural wrongs of our initial birth to open wide the mercy and grace of God.

It is this very church, then, that does not lack a toehold in the moral imperative of care for the poor and thoughtfulness about wealth—however misplaced—that is in the perfect place to adopt key tenets of ptoxocracy as it reconstitutes itself, tenets that would take her far beyond charity as meaningful stakeholders in the lives of the poor. What a vision for the future, if this church, already millions strong in members, declared itself a true stakeholder in the lives of the poor by way of shedding its holdings in the interests of the rich. To accomplish this, the church could take the most basic idea of ptoxocracy to practice—that is, to place an eligibility requirement of economic status on potential nominees for church leadership. A ptoxocratic alteration to the constitution would be a simple one: each congregation could decide for themselves what a ptoxocratic board might look like, whether at the poverty line, as land holders, or say, net worth that does not exceed a certain amount of money.

The first thing that I'm sure most communities would learn, my suburban context included, is that they would not be able to fill all the required positions on the board. This is an eye-opening reality. Howard Thurman's

Jesus and the Disinherited argues that the innermost nature of Jesus's movement speaks deeply to the lives of the poor, yet ptoxocracy would reveal that we have substantially missed the mark here. Congregations without enough individuals of ptoxocratic eligibility to maintain a board speaks as a deep indictment of the distance between the work of Jesus in the world and the church that hopes to continue his mission. In other words, we may be missing out on a fundamental segment of our constituency whose lives would be affected by the words, life, death, and resurrection of Jesus, and ptoxocracy could help us regain exactly this missing part.

In churches today one notices this distance in all sorts of expressions. When board leaders lament the reality of poverty now, they tend to imagine charity as its sole solution. As Thurman says, "No man wants to be the object of his fellow's pity."[11] This unimaginative solution to poverty in one's own community lacks relationship. Charity perpetuates the chasm between rich and poor, turning the rich into saviors while teaching the poor to be dependently grateful for scraps. Anyone who has sorted cans at the canned food drive knows plainly the shallow depths of charity. The problem of this chasm is one we have already argued, that the rich lack a true stake in the lives of the poor. As such, their imaginations fail, no matter how well-intentioned or true their aim at alleviating the reality of poverty.

Imagine, instead, a board whose members are all true stakeholders in the lives of the poor by the fact of their own poverty. Immediately one sees a church that takes a firm and consequential step back from the vestiges of the inherent plutocracy the Roman Empire bequeathed to the church as a structural given. In rejecting wealth as a prerequisite to power, the church would begin to empower the poor immediately. In consequence, by slightly altering the already democratic norms of governance in this way the church could drastically alter the access of poor persons to power in their civic communities. Where democratic processes tend to keep the poor out of power, the church could inject the materially poor into civic life by way of its own constitution. A civically active church, then, would be one in which poor voices have a collective platform to mobilize and draw attention to mistreatments known in the very communities they worship within.

Present movements in pastoral and theological training have highlighted the need of congregations and their leaders to function as community organizers, and ptoxocracy would add, rather than detract, from this movement. A great example of this is highlighted in the *New York Times*

---

11. Thurman, *Jesus and the Disinherited*, 36.

story of January 4, 2025, of the work of Pastor Katrina Foster of St. John's Lutheran Church in Brooklyn. Highlighting Foster's capacity to rebuild congregations throughout her career, the *Times* reporter went into the neighborhood in search of clues to her success when so many churches are closing. In contrast to a model of ministry that might have a pastor tucked safely into their studies preparing Sunday sermons, "[Foster] went door to door in the community, asking people what they needed and how she could help. When a school required money to fix holes in a fence, she helped call a news conference where she held up clear bags of used condoms and needles collected from the schoolyard." Clearly the methodologies of community organizing have helped Foster, whose congregation has grown nearly tenfold in half as many years. "When children were being hit by speeding cars, she called the Bronx Department of Transportation commissioner directly and implored him to install speed bumps."[12] Stories of pastors like Foster are not unique, and it is indeed heartening to see them lifted in national media outlets. Yet the authenticity of her ministry, supplemented by a ptoxocratic structure, would not only serve as a powerful witness in the world but demonstrate the effectiveness of centering institutions in the poor.

Returning to the earlier anecdote, a church board comprised of the *ptoxoi* would have treated my pastor friend differently, and I expect that she in turn would have treated the call to pastor the congregation differently. A group of the community's poorest persons serving as leaders would give vocal reality to the expense of life in that community in a way that the rich simply could not. The church in that community might become a refuge site for the poor rather than yet another organization quietly perpetuating bias and disdain of the poor. Whether that would have altered contract negotiations and raised her pay, who knows. But rather than a top-down decision in which she was told simply to get over it and do her job out of some theologically idealistic duty, she might have turned to the people around her and asked, "How is it that you manage to live in this wealthy suburb?" She probably would have heard stories. She probably would have heard about community, the kind of community that opens when people help and support one another in ways the rich can't understand in their wealth-induced myopic isolation. She probably would have had a fire stoked in her belly by the Spirit calling her into deeper relationship and solidarity with those whom she earnestly wanted to serve, a call that would have landed her at the doorstep of rich and poor alike. The poor do not scoff at

---

12. Krueger, "Church Fixer," para. 25.

poverty, for they know it is a deadly serious thing to ask another person to take on willingly. But instead, in her case, the rich board members scoffed at her requests for a living wage in their neighborhood, and she decided to move along to a pastoral call in a neighborhood she could afford.

Ptoxocracy would certainly draw attention to the church as authentic to its own values in a time when attention is lacking. Most of the young people I've served over the years tell me they struggle with the church because it doesn't seem to live into its own values in any meaningful kind of way, revealing a crisis of authenticity within organized Christianity. One of the most glaring disconnects between value and action is often perceived around issues of immigration, though the perception is not always a fair one, especially among churches working constantly to better the lives of new Americans. Speaking of her work among countless volunteers, advocates, and activists in this field, pastor and activist Helen Boursier notes how disaffected many of these passionate individuals have become from their former religious contexts because of the refusal to engage the moral crisis at hand. She writes that many say "their church's silence and inattention to the immigration crisis was so disheartening that they could no longer respect it for any ethical, moral, religious, or spiritual leadership."[13] The mere notion of a ptoxocratic church would turn the heads of these disaffected activists in the very least. A ptoxocratic church would instantly perceive the disconnect between a billboard that states "All Are Welcome" and a culture that recognizes informal hierarchies of citizenship status or birthplace as markers of cultural superiority. To become a ptoxocratic church would be to reauthenticate the structure of the church by way of its value systems.

CONCLUSION

Make no mistake that ptoxocratic changes to church constitutions would result in a wave of exits, though it's likely that those would most certainly not be its poorest members. Forced to follow the poorest among them, these departures would likely ask what most pastors already hear frequently: "What's money got to do with the church?" Such willful ignorance and forgetfulness of the many times Jesus speaks about wealth would continue to disappoint and astound. Money has a lot to do with church, but unfortunately, the loudest voices silencing the true role of wealth in the church are

---

13. Boursier, *Precious Precarity*, 7.

the rich. Shielded by the illusion of charity from the discomfort of Jesus's centering of the *ptoxoi*, the rich prefer a church that plays by the rules of the prefect of Rome rather than Lawrence, whose poor and disinherited may tarnish their buildings. I am hardly the first pastor to make this claim and will by no means be the last. Martin Luther King Jr., examining the way that early Christians like Lawrence challenged and put an end to structural evils of the Roman world, wrote, "The contemporary church is so often a weak, ineffectual voice with an uncertain sound. It is so often the arch supporter of the status quo. Far from being disturbed by the presence of the church, the power structure of the average community is consoled by the church's often vocal sanction of things as they are."[14] I am under no illusions: a ptoxocratic church might suffer a similar fate to Lawrence, and of King. It would likely mean the loss of social privilege, institutional wealth, and status.

Yet staring down crises of decline on multiple fronts spurred along by both growing trends of secularity and a crisis of authenticity whose tangible effects are hopelessness and anxiety, it's clear that the church could do much worse than a meaningful investment in the lives of the poor. Phyllis Tickle is well known among church leaders for her observation of a monumental shift in church dynamics—a reformation, in fact—that she argues arises in a loose set of five-hundred-year cycles.[15] Accepting Tickle's thesis of an overarching trend in Christian history as such or not, one cannot help but look around at the state of organized Christianity today and marvel at the changed landscape from even fifty years ago. Ptoxocracy could, and would, constitute a reformation of church structure of the magnitude and proportion of Tickle's thesis if the church would dare to implement its principal assertions into its own body.

Whether or not the rest of society followed in its footsteps toward ptoxocratic governance wouldn't matter, for such a church would reclaim the most authentic vision of itself and reembolden her mission. "Wherever the early Christians entered a town," wrote King, "the power structure got disturbed and immediately sought to convict them for being 'disturbers of the peace' and 'outside agitators.' But they went on with the conviction that they were 'a colony of heaven' and had to obey God rather than man. They were small in number but big in commitment. They were too God-intoxicated to be 'astronomically intimidated.'"[16] If the church hopes to

14. King, "Letter from a Birmingham Jail," 106–7.
15. Tickle, *Great Emergence*.
16. King, "Letter from a Birmingham Jail," 107.

reclaim its capacity for meaningful disturbance in the world, it must do so by way of structural authenticity. If Jesus was a ptoxocrat, then it follows that church structures ought to become ptoxocratic. Ptoxocracy, in other words, might help the church reclaim her own authentic voice.

There is no resurrection to life without death. Perhaps rather than salvage the remains of the church, it is time for our present embodiment of Christianity to end and to give rise to another.

7

The Ptoxocratic Lens

We've mistaken moral outrage for moral compass. Moral compass helps you see with clarity how complex and damaged people are. It is the whole language. Moral outrage just increases the volume and the distance that separates us. I suppose if I thought moral outrage worked, I'd be out raging.

— Greg Boyle, *The Whole Language*

Sitting around a campfire into the night in the Great Smoky Mountains last summer, I leaned into a conversation with an old friend and told him about ptoxocracy. A successful middle-management type with an oft-hidden penchant for the kinds of books that would raise the eyebrows of his business associates, he nodded along excitedly as I described the outline of the book I was writing. "What a fascinating thought experiment," he said. When I didn't answer, he prodded, "But that's all this is, right, a thought experiment?" I peered up at the stars one more time and considered his question. "You can't actually be serious about putting the poor in charge of things," he said.

On the one hand, I had to pause in response to his question because this book has a dimension that we might call a thought experiment. Indeed, this is how the project first began. Philosophers use thought experiments all the time as they imagine possibilities in the world. Socrates employed a thought experiment in Plato's *Republic* when he imagined a community of people living in a cave, subject to suffering under false illusions brought about by puppetry and shadows. Socrates then imagines that this figurative community of the cave is released into the wider world, and he wonders how and whether the members of this imagined group will be changed in their perspectives, what effect their post-cave lives might have on the world. Imagining a former cave-dweller dragged into the light of reality, Socrates asks his conversation partner, "Wouldn't he be pained and angry at being treated that way?"[1] Thought experiments allow philosophers to step inside an imagined world and play out their consequences and effects.

In a way, this book has been a thought experiment insofar as this is exactly what we've been doing until this point: imagining a world that does not exist, and observing the consequences of this imagined world based on our experiences of life within it. Ptoxocracy has yet to exist in its purest sense as a functional system of governance in any state or organization, so far as I can tell. Insofar as every philosophical idea in its pure form constitutes a thought experiment of sorts—that is, there are hardly any pure forms of any human systems—our project until now has indeed functioned as such.

Yet if this project existed only as a thought experiment then it would completely undermine the radically ptoxocratic assertion rooted in the heart of the Gospels. Jesus hardly treated the poor as a thought experiment, and the constant treatment of them as such has given rise to the state of things as we find it historically. In fact, it is exactly the treatment of the poor as a thought experiment that continues to decrease the stake held in the well-being of their lives at the hands of the rich. To treat the poor as anything but fully human ends in themselves is to fall short of Jesus's explicit goal to pronounce "good news to the poor" (Luke 4:18b).

Thankfully, ptoxocracy is not alone in the work of dignifying the *ptoxoi*; traces of the ptoxocratic impulse have already emerged within human systems, and continue to do so to this day. While a pure form of ptoxocracy places strict eligibility requirements on those seeking to become officeholders in either a state, church, or private group, a less pure form of ptoxocracy exists in the world already, and it is to this impure form of ptoxocracy in practice today that we turn to in conclusion. The aim of this chapter is to explore how and whether ptoxocratic principles, theological frames, and ideas have indeed been a part of civil discourse, particularly discourse within social justice movements of the last century, and to what extent the language and descriptive logic of ptoxocratic ideals helps hone that discourse for the better. Ptoxocracy becomes a lens through which

1. Plato, *Republic*, 209.

social justice advocates can more adequately describe the goals, barriers, and solutions to the challenges in dealing with issues of poverty.

PTOXOCRACY AS A LENS

We arrive, then, at ptoxocracy as descriptive language that falls within the frame of wider social justice discourses, and which may be employed to imbue a certain set of aims and problems with meaning, even in impure forms. In other words, the ideas explored already and contained within ptoxocracy can function as a particular lens or frame through which we can delineate actions, movements, ideas, challenges, and possibilities. For theologians and philosophers, the technical word here is *hermeneutic*. To paraphrase what we have seen in this book until now, these hermeneutical frames include (though may not be limited to) ptoxocratic assertions as the following:

- The rich hold no meaningful stake in the lives of the poor.
- The rich do not govern by divine right, nor are they any more capable of good governance than any other body of persons (the mythology of the rich ruling class).
- The poor can only rule if wealth and ruling political power are decoupled—one may seek wealth or representative political power, but not both at once.
- Any person can become poor, but not all persons can become rich.
- Within a representative democracy, the best way to ensure equal participation and stakeholding in the wider civic good is by way of an eligibility requirement based on economic standing.
- The poor rule the kingdom of God.

If we take these ideas to be the central themes of ptoxocracy which comprise a pure form of ptoxocracy in practice, then we can also say that these ptoxocratic principles can be found as impure forms within existing organizations. Identifying impure forms of ptoxocracy—that is, employing ptoxocracy as descriptive language—helps to build common cause among disparate factions. Ptoxocracy lends a communal language across social groups and activists who might otherwise find no common language in their shared goals. It is toward these projects that we now turn our attention, highlighting the ways that ptoxocracy gives language and clarity to such projects.

A Case Study in the Ptoxocratic Lens: Homeboy Industries

Homeboy Industries is a nonprofit organization in Los Angeles, California, whose core aim is to empower people to leave the gang lifestyle. In their own words, "Homeboy Industries provides hope, training and support to formerly gang-involved and previously incarcerated individuals allowing them to redirect their lives and become contributing members of our community."[2] Their eighteen-month flagship program, which serves about 450 such persons each year, serves clients with wraparound treatments that will help them reenter life as community members, alongside job training, healing, and mentoring. Twelve social enterprises and businesses ranging from cafes to screen printing shops to tattoo removal parlors provide job training opportunities for their clients, affectionately referred to as *homies* in both day-to-day language and within the many books about Homeboy. Homeboy Industries was founded by Jesuit Father Greg Boyle in 1998, who continues writing and speaking about his work at Homeboy and working within the organization to this date. His best-selling books *Tattoos on the Heart, Barking to the Choir*, and *The Whole Language* provide an incredible snapshot of Homeboy's impact in the community. The methodology of Homeboy is what Boyle calls "radical kinship."[3]

Homeboy Industries serves as an excellent example of a ptoxocratic organization in action, striving to move beyond tokenism in both its organizational structure and decision-making processes. Using source material from Boyle's work and a recent book by the organization's CEO, Thomas Vozzo, called *The Homeboy Way: A Radical Approach to Business and Life*, we can analyze how the structures, methods, decision-making processes, stories, and experiences of Homeboy Industries may or may not conform to ptoxocratic principles. This examination helps us to see the ways that ptoxocratic ideas already function in the world today, as well as the ways that ptoxocratic principles form part of what is truly remarkable about the organization, giving rise to the life-changing potential of Boyle's notion of radical kinship. Homeboy is not a religious nonprofit, and makes no claim to its structure as such, though the ptoxocratic principles on display

2. Homeboy Industries, "Fact Sheet."
3. Boyle, *Barking to the Choir*.

through their work embody many of the theological commitments and foundations of ptoxocracy as outlined in chapter 4 of this book.

Thomas Vozzo is a fascinating voice, if not an entirely accidental one, for the advocacy of ptoxocratic principles in action. A businessman by trade, and one whose background includes executive leadership among some of the nation's Fortune 100 companies, Vozzo is an unlikely candidate advocating for the kinds of ptoxocratic principles found here. Bringing his skills to a floundering Homeboy Industries in 2012 as its CEO, it's clear from his book that both Vozzo and Homeboy have been massively altered (and I would argue, changed for the better) in their engagements.

Vozzo's authority for these arguments stems from his experience as one who previously worked himself up the ladder into corporate boardrooms, meetings with political actors, and a partner of powerful wealthy financial interests. His perspective is particularly piercing (and interesting from the ptoxocratic perspective) because he remains staunchly committed to both capitalism and the classic idea of what he frequently refers to as the "American Dream." Example after example in his book demonstrate his frustration with Los Angeles power brokers, politicians, and bankers in their complete lack of concern for the poor, a lack of concern that arises because of the myopic nature of the systems they inhabit, a myopia he once shared.

He highlights an example of this frustration in an examination of Homeboy's banking relationships. After years of existing as a purely cash business, Homeboy's leadership green lighted Vozzo's efforts to begin a formal banking relationship in 2016. He writes, "Up until then, all [our bank account] did was deposit money; we had no credit-borrowing facilities at all. Now we have a credit line of two million dollars that helps us greatly."[4] Until 2020, that relationship worked as planned, and Vozzo's insights as a CEO helped to further the mission of Homeboy in substantial ways. In 2020, however, the economic calamity that arrived with the pandemic threatened the organization's capacity to function. It was for these realities that the federal government passed the Cares Act and created the Paycheck Protection Program (PPP), designed to employ local banks in helping organizations like Homeboy receive forgivable loans to stay afloat. Like many other small business and nonprofit leaders, Vozzo ensured that Homeboy's paperwork was ready for the first day of the loan's availability, and he was in regular contact with his banker to see that everything was set to go.

---

4. Vozzo, *Homeboy Way*, 151.

Yet on the day applications were to be submitted, the bank's online portal never opened. Later the bank's CEO issued a formal statement, saying that because of oversight complications with the federal government, it would not be participating in the program. "Here we are," he writes, "waking up Monday morning ready to send in our application, and realize that our bank is not going to be there for us in a time of crisis, at a time when we need our bank the most."[5] Having sat in boardrooms with a history of making those kinds of decisions, Vozzo's anger at Homeboy's financial vulnerability in that moment is palpable as he recounts the story: "The more I thought about it, I saw clearly what had been going on. The CEO of our bank knew that they were under stricter regulatory oversight than other banks. They used the PPP as an issue to pry away deeper oversight, using small businesses and nonprofits as pawns in their 'game of chicken' with the regulatory agencies."[6] He goes on:

> I know how it plays out in these boardrooms on Wall Street. Bankers sit back and game-theory the scenarios. They do their chess moves, they work on what would be best for them and their shareholders long-term. What's forgotten in this equation is what's best for their customers. In a time of national crisis, our bank could have done it differently. What they chose to do was ... [use] small businesses and nonprofits as pawns.[7]

Vozzo is a particularly fascinating voice because he contains both the experience of those executive-level boardrooms as well as the ptoxocratic impulse emerging from his time at Homeboy. Like most of us, his interests are mixed, and ptoxocracy as descriptive language helps us understand the contours of his situation, yet his time at Homeboy imbued him with a stake in the lives of the poor, and such a stake has enabled him to look back at his previous time in the financial industry afresh. Ptoxocracy helps us understand his perspective on systems that prioritize the interests of the rich. He understands the pervasiveness of the mythology of the rich ruling class, a story that insists that rich executive decision-makers who look after their own interests are doing ultimate good as such. Yet given a new stake in the lives of the poor and disenfranchised, Vozzo becomes awake to dynamics that he would have missed had he stayed a corporate executive, thereby challenging this mythology by way of personal experience. He sees plainly

5. Vozzo, *Homeboy Way*, 152.
6. Vozzo, *Homeboy Way*, 153.
7. Vozzo, *Homeboy Way*, 153.

how the decisions of wealthy executives and government officials claim the well-being of all in society, yet so narrowly benefit the rich in practice. His tangible stake in the lives of the poor gives him new eyes, new ptoxocratic eyes, that affect the ways he does business, helps his organization, and functions in society.

Vozzo writes about his former life as an executive and this blindness, all the demonizing and demeaning narratives—a version of the mythology of the rich ruling class among them—that make myopia among political and business leaders possible. Because of his holding a stake in the lives of the poor as Homeboy's CEO, he writes, "Now I've come full circle to work with the poor and demonized, I've come to understand how the rich *view* those in poverty and how the poor *experience* poverty. Especially how very differently the concepts of the American Dream and meritocracy are understood between those of the Two Americas—it's the greatest gap I've ever seen."[8] Remember, within ptoxocratic systems one may be rich and one may be powerful, but one may not be both at once. Vozzo's time at Homeboy bolsters this principle, demonstrating the ways that, once given the chance to become a stakeholder in the lives of the poor, the rich are capable of advancing their interests, which now include the interests of the poor.

Vozzo is most thrillingly ptoxocratic in his deep criticism of meritocracy, one version of the mythology of the rich ruling class, born out of his experiences at Homeboy. In a chapter of *The Homeboy Way* titled "Meritocracy Does Not Always Work," Vozzo walks readers through the ways that the organization selects one individual out of a pool of hundreds of candidates to be admitted into their flagship rehabilitation program. He quotes Boyle, remembering how dumbfounded he was in learning Homeboy's criteria in the early days of his time there. "What we do," Boyle tells him, "is 'reverse cherry-pick;' that is, we take the applicants who need it most. . . . We don't take the ones that Homeboy needs the most to improve our statistics."[9] Like Mary, the mother of Jesus, singing about a ptoxocratic world in which the rich will be made low and the poor lifted up, Homeboy's criteria for its flagship program is based on what Justo González calls the *great reversal*, the focus on those whom society has largely given up on. Their intention, as such, is a ptoxocratic one because it expresses the value of those poor persons whom society has discarded. It consciously lifts the

---

8. Vozzo, *Homeboy Way*, 155.
9. Vozzo, *Homeboy Way*, 96.

poor to the highest places in a world that forgets them. This is ptoxocracy in motion.

If Homeboy's mission stopped there it would be remarkable enough, yet the organization takes a step further into ptoxocracy: according to Homeboy's media fact sheet, more than two-thirds of its senior management are graduates of the flagship program. By many of the standards of Los Angeles, Vozzo admits that even these upper-management types still live in poverty. If we lived in a world of true meritocracy, the incredible accomplishments of these graduates would be met with wealth. Repeatedly Vozzo names the ways that the program's graduates remain disenfranchised in society, merely by the fact of their status as felons, skin color, accents, or their legal records as gang members. Many of these, whom he identifies as having the same potential and skill sets he had as an aspiring businessman, will never go on to encounter a world with the same opportunities as he did. Without the frame of ptoxocracy we might be tempted to call this a failure. Yet through the frame of ptoxocracy we can see the ways that the project is successful: Homeboy Industries organizationally manufactures a stake in the lives of the poor. By giving program graduates seats of actual authority within the program, Homeboy strides well beyond mere tokenism and into the actualization of ptoxocracy. Vozzo attests that the perspective of these graduate-managers is invaluable in helping Homeboy function with excellence.

In doing this, Homeboy's structures and leaders bolster claims to ptoxocratic forms, thereby undoing narratives, biases, and mythologies that continue to harm poor people. First, that ptoxocratic leadership—that is, leadership that holds a true stake in the lives of the poor—leads to higher functioning and better results within the organization than if Homeboy excluded the poor from among its organization's leaders. By reinvesting in graduates as potential leaders rather than hiring outsiders who may or may not have comparable skill sets, Homeboy proves that poor persons are capable. This seems like it should be a given. Indeed, as I write the words, I feel the discomfort of any implication that persons are incapable due to their economic status. Meritocracy, in its purist form, would prove this. Yet because meritocracy is indeed a mythology rather than a reality, it functions as a smokescreen that promotes the interests of the rich while suppressing the capacities of the poor, continuing to diminish the interests of the poor on behalf of the rich. Vozzo writes, reflecting on his experiences at Homeboy through the lens of Paulo Freire's *Pedagogy of the Oppressed*, that "oppressors work hard to keep the oppressed in their station in life, and thus the concept of the American Dream is a myth that keeps the oppressed placated."[10] In what could not be a more pure expression of ptoxocratic principles, he writes, "We [at Homeboy] are an antimeritocracy organization with an antimerit promotion system."[11] Homeboy's organizational structure provides evidence that ptoxocratic systems are not only possible, but work to better the organization itself. In other words, in a business landscape that insists that the only way to judge a person's value or worth is by economic standing (i.e., the corporate world's insistence on meritocracy), Homeboy proves the opposite: that the poor are just as capable, if not more capable, of running an effective organization.

It would be a drastic misevaluation to claim that Homeboy Industries represents a pure ptoxocratic organization. For instance, a majority of voting board members are not poor. Vozzo reminds readers that Homeboy's governing board, a group make up of Los Angeles economic elites, helped the organization during the pandemic PPP crisis. When their first bank failed them, Vozzo self-consciously remembers that while other nonprofit organizations in similar situations were not so fortunate, "[Homeboy] had 'elites' on our board, who could call other 'elites' to help us out. We knew the rules, how to play the game, and had some access to the game."[12] Because the purest expression of ptoxocracy would draw not only organizational leaders from among the poor as stakeholders, but as voting board members, it's clear that the organization is ptoxocratically incomplete. Moreover, while Thomas Vozzo does not draw a salary from his work as CEO of Homeboy, he is not a poor person and willingly admits that his capacity to employ his skill set there free of charge is only possible because of his independently earned wealth.

This would seem to disprove arguments about the inadequacy of charity found in chapter 1. One might argue that because wealthy elites both execute operations and govern Homeboy Industries, an organization that performs incredible social good in the world, that charity can meet the challenges of the world of poverty. Yet remember that the argument in chapter 1 is not that charity is incapable of meeting some of society's needs toward the poor, but that it is an inadequate way to meet all or even very many of the needs of the poor. As Vozzo reminds us, Homeboy's resources

10. Vozzo, *Homeboy Way*, 101.
11. Vozzo, *Homeboy Way*, 100.
12. Vozzo, *Homeboy Way*, 154.

only allow them to choose "one new trainee each week" for their flagship program, "out of a pool of more than two hundred community clients we may have at any given time."[13] Fascinatingly, though the organization selects those candidates whom it deems the most difficult (the philosophy of "reverse cherry-picking" as articulated by Boyle), Homeboy's rate of recidivism for formerly incarcerated persons is an astonishingly low 30 percent, while the city and county of Los Angeles, whose own budgets for projects that also aim to reduce gang participation tower over Homeboy's twenty-million-dollar budget, have recidivism rates of over 70 percent. Clearly something about the organization is working more efficiently than its counterparts, and I would argue that some of this has to do with its ptoxocratic nature.

This brings me to my final point about the relationship between ptoxocracy and Homeboy Industries. While Los Angeles City government functions within bureaucratic meritocracies whose structural form reduces the possibility for transformation among gang members by 30 percent, Homeboy's ptoxocratic principles accomplish something else entirely— namely, the radical kinship that Boyle writes about in his books. Radical kinship remains the primary methodology behind the success of Homeboy Industries. In the foreword to Vozzo's book, Boyle writes, "Homeboy Industries puts forward the idea that we need to build a system of care that offsets our over-built system of punishment."[14] Another book of theology could be written as an examination of Boyle's radical kinship and its effects, even outside the canon of Boyle's own work. Since radical kinship as a methodology is not our topic, however, I must stifle my theological and practical enthusiasm for this idea and let it suffice to say that radical kinship would not be possible for the organization without some form of ptoxocratic ideas underpinning the structural identity of Homeboy Industries. The ptoxocratic forms give rise to the potential for radical kinship.

In the final analysis, Homeboy proves to be a fascinating case of an incomplete, or impure, form of ptoxocratic principles in motion. Not only do its leaders understand the failures of meritocratic systems as a mythology, but they actively promote and employ ptoxocratic measures to counterbalance the failures of the myth. Moreover, while charity keeps Homeboy Industries open, seeming to pose a counterexample to the claims of charity's failure in chapter 1 of this text, the organization serves as an

---

13. Vozzo, *Homeboy Way*, 94.
14. Boyle, Foreword, vii.

example of a group that has broken through the failures of charity by way of ptoxocratic principles. No system functions purely in practice; given the landscape of what Vozzo calls the "Two Americas," one for the rich and one for the poor, Homeboy's accomplishments are impressive. Lastly, Vozzo's existence as Homeboy's CEO bolsters, not diminishes, ptoxocratic assertions, for within ptoxocracy one may be rich, and one may be powerful, but not both at once. While Vozzo's status as CEO would seem to contradict this statement, a deeper examination proves more intriguing: what is truly remarkable about Vozzo's relationship to Homeboy is that he is a rich person who has located a meaningful stake in the lives of the poor, and that his ptoxocratic stake has been transformational for both he and the organization. He has become a shareholder in the lives of poor persons, and this stake has been personally transformational and institutionally vital. Ptoxocracy does not assert that rich persons have no place in society or that they are inherently incapable of doing well by the poor. Rather, it estimates that society will never find real ways of ending, even addressing poverty without the presence of real stakeholders of the poor among the rich. Vozzo has proven that given the chance to hold a stake in the lives of the poor, rich persons hold a valuable place in society. His skills are vital to Homeboy's existence. In other words, the rich and the poor can coexist, and the rich can play an important role in the work of constructively addressing the needs of the lives of the poor, but this requires a mechanism by which the rich attain a meaningful stake in the lives of the poor.

Other Ptoxocratic Forms

Twentieth-century theologian and social activist Howard Thurman began his monumental *Jesus and the Disinherited* with the words, "The conventional Christian word is muffled, confused, and vague" to the poor of the world. "Too often," he writes, "the price exacted by society for security and respectability is that the Christian movement in its formal expression must be on the side of the strong against the weak."[15] These words, and the words that follow, have already inspired generations of Christians to reinhabit and reimagine a faith that contends with the unfortunate assimilation of Christianity into the structures of power. Ptoxocracy is also inspired by these, and wonders whether structural change rather than political movement might be needed in further disentangling faith from "security and

15. Thurman, *Jesus and the Disinherited*, 1.

respectability." It would be disingenuous, if not outrightly erroneous, to assert that others have not considered structural means for disentanglement prior to ptoxocracy. As we have seen though the examination of Homeboy Industries, structural changes to organizations are available prior to the formal examination of purely ptoxocratic assertions. To gain further clarity on the ways that ptoxocracy as language might be used as a frame or lens in evaluating and enabling social justice, it may be helpful to name a few others in brief. In this section we will briefly outline other examples of the ways that organizations, particularly the church, are already doing the work of ptoxocracy, and how employing the ptoxocratic lens allows us to see and recognize this work more clearly.

In December 2024, the Episcopal Church announced that their $500 million portfolio would be fully divested of fossil fuels. Anytime we witness the organizational impulse to recognize the impact and self-interest contained in the act of stakeholding, both in terms of holding stakes in a destructive operation in the world or in terms of holding a meaningful stake in the lives of the poor, one can see the first ptoxocratic assertion in motion. Sarah Lawton, chair of the denomination's Executive Council Committee on Corporate Social Responsibility, said of the move that "the Episcopal Church was an early leader in the global movement to consider ethical criteria and faith commitments, and also long-term risk assessments, in investment and portfolio decisions, starting with our work to oppose apartheid in South Africa in the 1970s."[16] The drive to root the ethical decisions of an explicitly Christian organization within the teachings of Jesus is not explicitly ptoxocratic in nature. However, the act of identifying economic self-interest through stakeholding powers is explicitly ptoxocratic in nature. Because the worst effects of climate change are already wreaking havoc on the world's poorest communities, the Episcopal Church is effectively divesting from those interests that most obviously damage the lives of poor persons. Moreover, the divestment is ptoxocratic action insofar as it recognizes that not all persons—or in this case, organizations—can become rich, but all can become poor. The divestment may not make sense in terms of traditional understandings of shareholder values, stock returns, and portfolio management, so that it is a willing step into the possibility of poverty for the sake of the poor. As such, the church gains a meaningful stake in the poor.

---

16. Paulsen, "Episcopal Church Completes Divestment," para. 7.

Another example concerns a church body whose methodology in dealing with poor communities has been reoriented, from that of fixing or saving the poor, to accompanying them and learning to become mutual shareholders in their well-being. Several years ago, the Evangelical Lutheran Church in America took steps to reorient its verbiage and practices around missional activities in third world nations in ways that are also ptoxocratic in nature. In shifting missional activities from the more traditionally understood perspective, "bringing God's story to the faithless heathens" (who often live in poor nations, as it happens), the church began employing the language of accompaniment. Shifting the perspective from a top-down narrative, often pejorative and diminutive in nature, to a model of walking beside already formed and dignified persons, the church made a ptoxocratic shift insofar as it took steps in undoing the mythology of the rich ruling class. Because divisions between the ELCA (a church in America—that is, the Global North) and the outside world often took the unintentional form of rich foreigners bringing resources to poor persons in the Global South, traditional missionary practices, whether intentionally or not, perpetuated a form of the mythology of the rich ruling class. Writing on her experiences within the ELCA's Young Adults in Global Mission program, a ministry of the ELCA originally modeled after the US Peace Corps, Rachel Swenson says of accompaniment, "We are not sent to fix, to change, or to rectify. . . . We are sent to listen to those who may feel voiceless, sent to shoulder some of the weight of impossible burdens if we can and sent to be continually awed and humbled by our experiences within our new homes. We are sent to be filled—with the good and the bad."[17] The shift from fixing to walking alongside is ptoxocratic in nature because it insists on the dignity of the *ptoxoi* in and of themselves, thereby undoing the mythology of the rich ruling class. Further, the shift to accompaniment language decouples wealth from power: the poor are given power and dignity over the course of their lives, rather than receiving goods, services, and dollars in exchange for obedience.

One final example highlights the ways that ptoxocratic language might illuminate the shared aims of bettering the lives of poor people to foster a spirit of collaboration where there is now a problematic animosity. This example pertains to the relationship between the church (at large) and social justice organizations such as Black Lives Matter (BLM). As a clergyperson within a predominantly white demographic, I can attest to

---

17. Swenson, "On Accompaniment," para. 3.

the number of misrepresentations of BLM within the church, even if many representatives of my denomination (pastors and national leaders) openly support the organization. It's no accident that a pair of BLM's founding organizers, Patrisse Khan-Cullors and Asha Bandele title their book *When They Call You a Terrorist: A Black Lives Matter Memoir*. They write, "There was a petition that was drafted and circulated all the way to the White House. It said that we were terrorists."[18] BLM is not a terrorist organization, yet many churches have succumbed to believing ugly rhetoric about their mission.

At the risk of employing a label that they may suffer under once again—for the adversaries of social justice are excellent at turning labels into violence—their project contains traces of the ptoxocratic. The refrain heard in 2020 protests, "black lives matter" (which transformed into an organization of the same name, Black Lives Matter), contains an explicitly ptoxocratic element. Insofar as racial inequality and economic inequality are intermingled issues of social justice, the mere presence of "matter" imbues the protest utterance with a ptoxocratic frame: namely, that there are persons in this world whose lives do not matter to other persons. This is a racial reframing of the ptoxocratic assertion that the rich hold no meaningful stake in the lives of the poor.

Ptoxocracy helps the church understand its shared cause with organizations like BLM, building a bridge where there is otherwise distrust. Using theological language rooted in the words of Jesus as rhetorical cover, if a white member of my congregation asks me why I support BLM (supposing that ptoxocracy as a category of language has permeated my community as a theological good rooted in the Gospels), I might now point to BLM as a generally ptoxocratic organization, rooted in or aligned with the Gospels, and therefore in line with our own congregation's aims as a fellow ptoxocratic organization. This is why emphasizing ptoxocracy's deep roots within the Christian tradition is such a powerful move within Christian communities, because it fixes the idea within a set of sacred texts and rituals held by a wide population of persons (namely, white Christian Americans) who are overwhelmingly—and bafflingly—opposed to organizations like BLM. Ptoxocratic language gives rise to the possibility of interpreting the actions of BLM through the lens of Christianity, widening it to a population that may be more sympathetic to its aims once connected concretely with the elements of faith. This is not to dominate or confuse BLM as a Christian

---

18. Khan-Cullors and Bandele, *When They Call You A Terrorist*, 6.

organization, but to share in recognition of common cause and to become allies. If Jesus was a ptoxocrat, then seeking common ground with non-Christian organizations like BLM is an easy move toward bettering the lives of those whom Jesus centers.

False Ptoxocracy: Tokenism

At their best, diversity and inclusion efforts among power structures, say, among leaders on nonprofit organizational boards, are indeed ptoxocratic in nature. Many organizations are aware of the myopia of board leadership when all members arrive with a similar set of backgrounds, ethnicities, sexualities, genders, ages, races, and economic statuses. What is ptoxocratic in the idea of diversity is the notion that economic diversity matters among power brokers. If ptoxocracy insists the rich hold no meaningful stake in the lives of the poor, then a governing board of any sort that opens a voting share of power to an economically disadvantaged person is employing a kind of ptoxocratic principle. They are, at best, attempting to give itself a stake in the lives of poor persons. At their worst, sometimes these efforts are expressions of tokenism, such that the diversity expressed is mere show of good public relations or shallow political appropriateness.

An example here helps. I currently sit on a board of directors for a church-affiliated organization that holds yearly elections for several at-large positions. The year after I was elected, we identified diversity as a strong growth edge and were intentional to ensure that the following year's slate of nominations would be more socioeconomically, linguistically, economically, and professionally diverse. While our constitution mandated a certain number of those standing for election be ordained pastors, many of whom tend to be white and male in our area, we were confident that we could find a slate of diverse candidates to fill the other positions. We celebrated, therefore, when one of the incoming board members, a Latina woman from a predominantly Spanish-speaking neighborhood, was an hourly restaurant worker. Her election felt like a real success for us, as we recognized that identifying and removing the blind spots that orient the business and priorities of church organizations toward predominantly white and affluent communities required diverse stakeholders be elected to positions of authority. The board meets quarterly, and it's unfortunate to say that she's never been able to attend a meeting in the three years since her election. One might be tempted to point to her attendance record as anecdotal evidence that diversity efforts like these are generally fruitless, or—worse—that a person of her socioeconomic class is incapable of handling the kinds of responsibilities that board leadership requires. These are troubling explanations, but unfortunately some I've heard spoken by fellow board members.

The explanation is a bit more straightforward, I think, and serves to highlight the ways that church organizations are oriented toward the expectations of and within predominantly wealthy communities. Our assumptions about where and when to meet, how to meet, and the organizational structure take on the assumptions of life within the middle to upper classes of the United States. First, the board meets on Saturdays. Saturdays are important days for an hourly-wage worker in the restaurant industry. If we met in-person on a Monday morning (her day off), for example, I wonder whether she would be able to meet more often. What's more, it might even work for the others on the board: even though this is a workday for many of us, the majority of board members are professionals whose work schedules affords flexibility, if not paid time off. Saturdays would require her taking time off, and if we know anything about restaurant work, paid time off is a benefit that even salaried management struggle to receive. Second, the board usually meets in church fellowship halls across the region, and getting to these various locations can take three hours or more from some areas of the region. Thankfully the organization will pay mileage reimbursement to anyone who requests it, but the time commitment away from family (especially her young children) in getting to meetings is a barrier. These are just two of many reasons why she hasn't been able to attend board meetings, and they demonstrate the ways that structures of our board are set up to accommodate the daily realities of the rich. The board takes it as a given that members can afford childcare, and that certain days of the week are restful, both of which are assumptions common among the rich.

Without intention or malevolence, the daily assumptions of the rich become the de facto arbiter of how we organize. Yet it is not just church boards that mistake the day-to-day assumptions of the rich as common to all. I frequently hear other pastors both within and outside of my denomination frustrated that church attendance is lagging on Sunday mornings, usually pointing a finger at encroaching time commitments like youth soccer leagues, a favored, though erroneous, bogeyman of church decline. This assumption however betrays yet another way that the lifestyles and priorities of the rich dominate discourse: those who can afford expensive traveling youth soccer teams are rarely the poor. I would invite church leaders struggling with Sunday morning attendance to avoid pointing fingers at soccer leagues and sporting events, and to rather follow their worshipping members out the door to brunch after morning worship to see where a far greater problem lies. There they'll find all manner of hourly-wage workers whose schedules are dictated by the whims of the rich. Do you like being able to pump gas on the way to worship? Great! There's a wage worker behind the counter who won't be in worship. Did the altar guild forget to restock the wine, and so head to the grocery store first thing Sunday morning to pick up a bottle of Manischewitz? Great, there's a staff of workers there too who won't be in church. All this is to say that the very structures that we employ, even in organizations whose explicit aim is to do good in the world, stymie the very work of justice we seek to achieve. Without an actual diversity of stakeholders on governing boards, one with the authority of decision-making within representative bodies, institutions like the church will continue making decisions based on the normative expectations of the rich. To be blind to these is to lay fault in all the wrong places, which is why the ptoxocratic frame becomes imperative. If there ever was an organization that understood the need to center the lives of the poor, it ought to be the church.

When the best we can imagine for the poor comes down to an economic tokenism, one must conclude that we do not care much to be a church that includes the poor. So long as the church expects the poor to conform to the social expectations of the rich, the poor will not be a part of the church. So long as my board continues to meet on Saturdays and expect volunteers to commute a few hours across the region, pay for childcare out of pocket, or stay overnight to participate in meetings—aspects of our work together that are generally well-accepted by the professional volunteers present—we can expect that our newest board member will not be present. Her lack of presence will reinforce our biases and continue to leave her voice outside of decision-making processes.

While the problems of tokenism have been highlighted in board leadership among for-profit and nonprofit organizations, the instinct toward economic diversity among board leadership is indeed a ptoxocratic one. While strict ptoxocracy understands that the only way to ensure a full stake in the lives of the poor is to completely disentangle wealth from power, the explicit inclusion of economically disadvantaged persons among governing boards is an important step toward creating a more equitable society at large. However, for these assignments to be truly meaningful, a board needs to recognize the ways that its forms (meeting times, insider language, assumptions, etc.) serve to reduce the participation of poor persons. Until boards make conscious efforts to meet the schedules of the *ptoxoi*, for example, there is little chance for the board to have a meaningful stake in the lives of the poor. Thankfully there is a trend among nonprofits who have moved in the direction of constitutionally mandated board seats drawn from populations of persons they're serving. One church in my area that serves hot meals to unhoused populations, along with other goods and services, for example, has modified their by-laws so that no fewer than one board position goes to a current or former client of the organization. Again, the effectiveness of these positions will be gauged through the degree to which they give the board a meaningful stake in the lives of those whom they serve by way of this board member. Such effectiveness can be measured by the basic standard of whether the member in that seat is able to attend meetings at all, and whether their seat raises a board's stake in the lives of the community served.

All this is to say that there are some charity groups and nonprofits who employ ptoxocratic aims but fall short, those that embody ptoxocratic assertions and meet these aims in a less-than-pure way, and others that fail to aim toward ptoxocratic assertions altogether. In the latter case, there are, to be sure, enormously beneficial organizations whose governing bodies care little for ptoxocracy. The argument here is not that a failure to include ptoxocratic aims is ineffective. Rather it is to say that there are some effective organizations that employ these, and some that do not. Merely being a nonprofit or charity, in other words, does not classify an organization, person, or structure as ptoxocratic in nature.

CONCLUSION

We could go on at length in observing other case studies in ptoxocratic forms, but these few help to illustrate the point. Ptoxocracy is novel only insofar as it gives language to a particular subset of assertions within the larger work of social justice. It's not as if activists have been blind to the challenges of poverty until now; quite the opposite. Moreover, many organizations have sought to give the rich a stake in the lives of the poor without ptoxocratic language. Yet this common language and set of frames can be helpful because it parses out interests more clearly and helps organizations locate the impulse within possible coworkers. What is not ptoxocratic is the idea that the rich have the capacity to fix, solve, or help poor persons by sheer will of force, means of charity, or because of their particular intellect or insights, or that a present course that continues to perpetuate a system whereby the de facto leadership of boards and governments is largely made up of the rich is doing much of a job. These examples, though they are few, demonstrate an instinct within the Episcopal Church, the ELCA, and small nonprofits that have all come to recognize that it is practically impossible to make a meaningful and positive change in the lives of poor persons without holding a meaningful stake in their lives.

In all three examples we see a ptoxocratic impulse that recognizes the harm of the unexamined relationship between wealth and power. The unexamined coupling of wealth and power gives rise to the myopic illusion that the wealthy and powerful alone have the capacity to fix or solve the challenges of poverty, as if the dignity of poor persons in making life-altering decisions were nonexistent. In the words of Jeffrey Stout once again, "Power minus accountability equals domination."[19] These organizations demonstrate something of a minimal form of ptoxocracy insofar as they recognize that the unexamined relationship between wealth and power regarding the poor has resulted in forms of domination that they cannot, and will not, tolerate any longer. Such an intolerance of the domination of the poor is ptoxocratic in nature.

---

19. Stout, *Blessed Are the Organized*, 55.

Conclusion

An End to Christianity

MOST IDEAS ARE NOT NAMED by the people who first theorize about them, but by their adversaries. I imagine that enemies of ptoxocracy will not be able to resist the proximity of the word "toxic" in English. "Ptoxocracy" they'll say, "it sounds awfully *toxic*," raising their eyebrows cleverly. Critics will intentionally misname it *toxocracy* in writing, wondering aloud whether the words are related though they are not. Rhetoricians will draw a clever line between the idea of ptoxocracy and its toxicity. It might be low hanging fruit, but it would be a powerful move. It would play upon the fears of loss of status quo, stability, and economic standing.

But that *p* is important. *Toxic* also has its roots in Greek, as it happens, and it means what we imagine it would mean. Something to do with poison, that which cannot be consumed else it might consume us.

The *p* in *ptoxocracy* is intentional. To speak the word is to perform its meaning. To pronounce a *p* immediately followed by a *t* one must let a touch of spittle emerge from the mouth. In other words, one must perform the very action of spitting to speak the word, a one-two step implicating the lips and the tongue in their willful collusion. The performance of *ptoxoi* is the act of perceiving its meaning. The pronouncement reenacts a common encounter, the true encounter of disdain known by the *ptoxoi* themselves.

A relatively easy line of attack against ptoxocracy comes in the form of an equalitarian argument, stating that any system or adjustment to democracy that limits rather than expands democratic participation is a step backward rather than forward. Since ptoxocracy technically limits democratic participants via eligibility requirements, this line of argument is justified. Yet the equalitarianism of this line of attack is both insincere and invalid. At the very least, one must ask their conversation partners to look squarely toward historical evidence bearing exactly the opposite. Meritocratic institutions hiding behind equalitarianism as a front to plutocratic ends are facts hiding in plain sight. Revisiting the words of Greg Boyle, the COVID pandemic revealed that inequality is not a defect in the system, *it is the system*.[1] No matter how many institutions hide behind meritocratic ideals, the *ptoxoi* know the belittlement within this mispronunciation well. Critics will not dare to perform this word as the motion toward its idea, for fear of literally wearing it on their chins. They'll have to rename it *toxocracy* to dissolve the collusion of their ideas with the time-honored tradition embedded in their defense.

But the word *ptoxocracy* itself, a word that leaves spittle upon the chin when properly pronounced, entails the emergence of an intentional cleaving. It could provoke a permanent severing of the connection between power and wealth. It is the idea that the rich are not entitled to power. It is the idea that the wealthiest among us do not, in fact, make the best of rulers. It is the idea that they, perhaps, make awful rulers and are best at serving only their own interests at the exclusion of the interests of society. It is the idea that to truly reach good governance we might need to rid governance of the interests of the wealthy as the primary aim of governance. It is the idea that the interests of the poor are equally important to the interests of the rich, perhaps (if we take Jesus seriously) even greater. It is a visionary challenge to the status quo as daring and dangerous as John of Patmos's vision of "a new heaven and a new earth" (Rev 21:1) devoid of imperial violence. To pry political power and wealth apart from one another as exchangeable currencies of power leaves us scratching our heads in bewilderment. How have we let these two become brothers, when indeed they are not? What would the world be like, what might democracy look like, if we could sever the connection?

I cannot think of a more timely question. Of course some will try to pronounce *ptoxocracy* without the *p*, for to pronounce that first letter is to pronounce a history of entitlement to the connection between power and wealth, a history that imbues the mythology that power earns wealth, and wealth brings political purchasing power, as both necessary and inevitable. They would sever it, because severing the word is much less dangerous than letting the implicit bond of wealth and power weaken. Mythologies are powerful forces.

---

1. Boyle, *Whole Language*, xi.

CONCLUSION

In the final assessment, ptoxocracy serves as a system capable of achieving a meaningful stake in the outcome of the lives of the poor. One who entertains ptoxocracy for a moment begins to see the world through its disdain for the poor, thus it accomplishes the unsettling severance of the givenness of power and wealth at least within the imagination. In conversations about property and community, one sees the spittle emerge from the mouths of wealthy interests as they speak about the destitute poor as a plague upon society, a plague that they themselves have no responsibility toward righting except by way of the scraps of tax-deductible charity. Once ptoxocracy imagines a system of governance in which the rules of the game are not so fundamentally skewed toward the rich, one begins to question why any society should be allowed to accept the rich as rightful rulers. Ptoxocracy, in questioning the mythology of the rich ruling class, begins to accomplish its task merely in the imaginative work itself.

Why do we allow the rich to swallow up not only goods but power? The words of Étienne de La Boétie, whose writing stands in contradiction to the Machiavellian writings of his age, are as apt today of the rich as they were of the tyrants they were written for in his own day in the sixteenth century:

> He who thus domineers over you has only two eyes, only two hands, only one body, no more than is possessed by the least man among the infinite numbers dwelling in your cities; he has indeed nothing more than the power that you confer upon him to destroy you. Where has he acquired enough eyes to spy upon you, if you do not provide them yourselves? How can he have so many arms to beat you with, if he does not borrow them from you? The feet that trample down your cities, where does he get them if they are not your own? How does he have any power over you except through you? How would he dare assail you if he had no cooperation from you? What could he do to you if you yourselves did not connive with the thief who plunders you, if you were not accomplices of the murderer who kills you, if you were not traitors to yourselves?[2]

Boétie's words smack timelessly against the shores of government in servitude of the rich, of governance whose aim is the interests of the wealthy. The aim of ptoxocracy is the liberation of government from not only their interests, but the violence of their whims.

---

2. La Boétie, "Discourse of Voluntary Servitude," 188.

Outside an examination of particular expressions of ptoxocratic impulses in the preceding chapter, I have said very little about other concrete anti-poverty projects, not to mention the hundreds of thousands of community organizers, activists, labor organizers, sociologists, academics, and others who comprise a broad and deeply concerned base that seeks the betterment of poor people. While I have pointed to Matthew Desmond's *Poverty, by America*, a treasure trove of practical solutions, I have intentionally stayed away from delving into the kind of concrete proposals that he and any group of sophisticated, nuanced, research-based, empirically measurable and studied ideas seek to explore. This has been by design. Fantastic ideas for ending poverty are all around us, and the citizens of the richest nation in the world have not only the intellectual skill but motivated leadership to accomplish the task. We are a nation rich in intelligence and capacity, leadership, and vision. This nation has more than enough movers, shakers, advocates, and activists to carry out the measured and excellent solutions to the reality of the misery and desperation of poverty. What we lack is the will of lawmakers to carry out these proposals. What we lack is a representative government that holds a meaningful interest in the lives of poor people. What we lack is a democratic system that demands that lawmakers hold an actual stake—a vested interest beyond normative kindliness and charity—in the lives of the poor. Without such a stake, no matter how intelligent and evidence-based our solutions might be, no matter how visionary or prophetic our leaders might be, history bears out the sad truth that this nation will continue in its ignoble forgetfulness of the poor. Let not the needy be forgotten, begs the psalmist.

True, certain lawmakers in the last hundred or so years stand head and shoulders above the fray, who are deeply concerned about the poor. Yet these are the minority. Today's American democracy continues to exist as a mechanism for the enrichment of those whose interests are most well-represented by elected officials: the rich. The clear majority of rulers of this land have no stake in the lives of the poor, so that, while they are democratically elected to stand as representatives for the poor and rich alike, they tend to best represent only the interests of the latter. Until representation for the poor happens in meaningful ways, I am certain that no matter how many excellent policy ideas we have, how many well-studied and decent proposals for civilized society we put forth, the government will continue to function as if the aims of its stakeholders, the wealthy, are its only goals.

CONCLUSION

The poor will continue to be an annoyance, a consequence, an afterthought, because the rich simply have no stake in the well-being of their lives.

Ultimately this is precisely the aim of this project: to inject a new idea into the bloodstream of the American experiment so potent that it might finally help those same lawmakers gain a stake in the lives of the poor. Ptoxocracy may be an awkward word, forcing a bit of spittle upon the face of a listener with each utterance, but the instant we inject it as an option into the conversation about potential of representative government, things can change. In a democratic society, lawmakers are quickly moved to action when constituents mobilize and coalesce around an idea. There is no threat like the threat of losing one's job as an elected official to spur a lawmaker to action. It is here that the mere idea of ptoxocracy may be enough, though I remain unsure of the extent of this claim. If American voters truly wished to see poverty ended, then the mere threat of ptoxocracy could be enough to begin to shift the tide. In other words, the idea itself may become a means by which the rich hold a stake in the lives of the poor.

Practically speaking, ptoxocracy functions as a methodology, a preamble you might say, to accomplishing the tasks that great thinkers like Desmond set forth. Theirs is the theory of how we might go about the business of change in this nation to care more about the poor and live into a more just society; ptoxocracy is the method of getting to the theory. By threatening lawmakers with a loss of power at the hands of ptoxocracy, we begin to give lawmakers a stake in the lives of the poor. By injecting a new language, a new threat into societal discourse—that is, the idea that the wealthy make for bad rulers and that we ought to place poor people in positions of authority (with the eventual goal of all positions filled by the poor)—we fashion an on-ramp to successful implementation of good policy where none exists now. In other words, the mere injection of the idea of ptoxocracy as a viable path toward governance could be enough to shift the political landscape in such a way that might finally begin to favor the poor.

Perhaps this is what Jesus meant to accomplish in blessing the poor during his sermons. I doubt very much that he only lifted these ideas up once in his preaching on plains or mountains, and imagine that they were central to his conception of the nearness of the kingdom of God. Certainly, there are traces of these sermons in every moment of the Gospels, but they are not ideas unique to him. Some theologians go so far as to remind us that it is Mary, a good Jewish daughter, who utters these well before Jesus, and that he may have learned them from her. The Hebrew Bible speaks plainly about God's concern for the poor, the alien, the widow, and the orphan; Mary's song is a timelessly raw expression of what God has been about since the waters of creation. By lifting God's preferential option for the poor, by preaching of the poor as rulers of this or any dominion belonging to God, Jesus means to lift them into the conversation and give the rest of humanity a stake in the outcome of their lives. This would be a hopeful thing indeed, not only for the poor, but for all of us who forget them. A body of his followers who would take it seriously might infuse the idea into local politics. A few thousand years have gone by, but it is not too late. I belong to a church, a body of the followers of Jesus, who have long been caught up in the mechanisms of empire, who have waved off Jesus's blessing for the poor as deluded at best, and sincere but ineffective at worst. Ptoxocracy invites us onto a new path.

END, ENDS, AND THE END

There are two primary ways that we can speak of *ends*: as a termination, and as an aim.

The first is to speak of an end as termination, as in the statement that "we are nearing the end of this book." This sense of the end signifies a point of closure or a finality. When a great film flashes the words "The End" on the screen, the audience understands that the plot has concluded within the frame of the work. This is also the sense that is communicated by *Terminus*, pagan god of boundaries, the angry Roman deity whose theological terror kept centurions from retreating from their posts on the frontiers in the face of barbarian invasion. When a medical professional writes the hour and minute on a death certificate, they mean an end in precisely this manner, as a point of expiration or death. When I tell my son to stop watching cartoons and eat his breakfast before school, I mean precisely an end in this way, too. We can speak of an end as a punctuation, either on a life or simply of a moment within life. This is an end as a point of finality or termination.

In the second sense, an end can be the thing toward which we point, or an aim. The bearings of a ship at sea come not from the waves or the landscape far beneath its hull, but from a point on the horizon in its relation to the stars. The captain aims the ship in a direction to the exclusion of all other directions, one degree among 359 other possibilities. Defining a particular end gives rise to a powerful tool in navigating the complexities of the world, a myriad of infinite possibilities that form a labyrinth of confusion and anxiety. Biomedical ethicists employ the word *end* in exactly this manner when interrogating a particularly sticky issue that a new technology or treatment yields, for example, asking whether the end (as a goal, an aim, or an outcome) is one that justifies a means of reaching it. This is what theologians and philosophers mean when they employ the term *teleology*, or the examination of ends.

Ptoxocracy is an end to Christianity in both senses of the word. When Jesus proclaims good news to the poor (Luke 4)—that is, that he aims for their betterment and inclusion within the grace of God—he articulates one end to his movement. It is possible to hold multiple aims, or multiple ends, in tension all at once. By way of example, during church board meetings it is not uncommon that a board member will suggest spending funds in a certain way, and inevitably another member in the room will responsibly ask, "Toward what end?" In this way, we mean *end* in the teleological sense, a fixed point that helps to orient, toward which a group or entity might aim collectively, even if it doesn't necessarily express itself as the totality of all ends. That same church board, for example, can at once identify both youth ministry and end-of-life-care to the elderly as ends, simultaneously. This means that they are both central to the work of the church, even if they aim in seemingly contradictory directions, that is toward the old and the young all at once. It is exactly in this way that Jesus can pronounce his aims as bringing good news to the poor and bringing about liberation for the captives without holding a contradiction. While the term *end* can feel exclusive when employed in this teleological sense, we are free to follow the lead of Jesus and employ multiple ends at once in just this sense. It is precisely this sense that I mean to say that Jesus centered the poor within his earthly ministry—that is, their betterment and inclusion within the grace of God was an end to his ministry, an aim.

It is a much more anxious thing to contemplate the end of Christianity as termination, even if the totality of that end is of a monumental scope. More clearly, what individuals and bodies of Christians mean when they employ the end of Christianity in this sense is the termination of their particularities within the wider discourse. North American Lutheran Christians often speak about the particularity of the Lutheran witness—that is, a particular set of ideas, theological convictions, tools, and traditions that comprise the whole of a reforming movement within the universal church. The anxiety raised in speaking of termination, therefore, is not of the end of

Christianity at large, but of a strain of human interpretations, stories, ideas, and institutions that signify something, like Lutheranism. Fascinatingly, we can observe that the totality of these strains within the wider frame of Christianity come to represent something of an end in the second sense—that is, that these particularities (say, Lutheranism or Presbyterianism) form an umbrella of terms, interpretations, and organizations that constitute an aim. In this way we see how the two senses of *end* are mutually informative.

In our anxiety to stave off the effects of these ends amid institutional decline and burnout, there is a central conviction that is easy to forget—that is, the faithfulness of God. To speak of a decline in Christianity is not to speak of a decline in the reality of the Holy Trinity or the unending grace of God. Anxiety forgets that what we speak of as ends in relationship to Christianity are not the subjects of Christianity themselves but the values, ideas, or commitments of persons within the human tradition constituted as church. In other words, the faithfulness and unending love of God will persist whether there is a single person who calls themselves a Lutheran or Presbyterian (or even Christian, for that matter). The power and reality of God are not dependent on our faithfulness.

So it is that we come to see that what persists in our anxiety is not an attachment to the Divine in its own right, but an attachment to the human structures that have come to represent the collections of ideas around God, structures that are both impermanent and subject to fault. To say it plainly, what we fear is not an end to God but an end to an -ism that has helped shape our own ideas, identities, and opinions about God. These are important, no doubt. But it is this very anxiety, deeply rooted within our own attachments to ourselves and not to God, that keeps us from imagining the world of possibilities beyond the single aim on our horizon—that is, the maintenance of a particular institution, the survival of a particular strain of theology, and so on. What's more, or possibly worse, depending on one's particular investment in the tradition itself, is that the enduring, unending faithfulness of God may be calling us to the work of releasing exactly these sorts of attachments. This is exactly how I interpret the words of the apostle Paul to the Philippians, when he invites his listeners to the imitation of Jesus, "who, though he existed in the form of God, did not regard equality with God as something to be grasped, but emptied himself" on the cross (Phil 2: 6–7a). Moreover, in attending to the imitation of Christ as one who let go of exactly these kinds of attachments—that is, his embodied self—Paul invites the reader to examine their interests: "Let each of you look not to your own interests, but to the interests of others" (2:4). Ptoxocracy invites the imitation of Christ by way of the examination of our interests, both as a collective institution as well as individuals.

This is precisely what is meant by ptoxocracy as an end to Christianity. Steeped in the salvific reality of God's mercy and love, to imitate Christ is to imitate the priorities of his earthly ministry in a way that empties ourselves of institutional preconditions or commitments. "The Spirit of the Lord is upon me, because he has anointed me to bring good news to the poor ... to proclaim release to the captives and recovery of sight to the blind, to let the oppressed go free" (Luke 4:18). Later, in the same Gospel, John's disciples approach Jesus, asking on the Baptizer's behalf, "Are you the one who is to come, or are we to wait for another?" (7:19), to which Jesus responds by articulating the central aims of his mission once again: "Go and tell John what you have seen and heard: the blind receive their sight, the lame walk, the lepers are cleansed, the deaf hear, the dead are raised, the poor have good news brought to them" (7:22). Surely followers of Jesus, while there are many aspects of faithful discipleship, hope to center his own explicit aims within our own practice of devotion. In other words, it seems logical that in becoming disciples of Jesus, the aims of Jesus's ministry ought to align, at least in some part, with the aims of our own. Yet what is unsettling about the historical church as we find it today is precisely the absence of what is central to Jesus's project—namely, the centering of the poor.

If charity toward the poor has failed to embody Jesus's call to this pronouncement of good news, will the church rise to empty itself in gain of its soul, or will it sink back into the depths of self-preservation? If the answer is that we will not rise, then we can aptly speak of the church today as a termination of Christianity insofar as the priorities of its subject—that is, Christ—are no longer the priorities of its own institutions. On the other hand, if the answer is to choose to rise, then the realization of a new structure is inaugurated, something that will look wholly different from the tradition as we have inherited it. This, again, is precisely what is meant by ptoxocracy as an end to Christianity, both as an aim and its terminus. The divestment of church from the constraints of rich rulers and its reinvestment in the poor would be of such enormous consequence that it would both significantly redirect the institution and christen a wholly new one at once.

The call of the church today is to the imitation of Christ, to pour ourselves out for the sake of the world that God so loves by way of meaningful investment in the lives of the poor by way of their elevation to ruling authority. The call of the church is ptoxocracy, either as a witness and practitioner or as its ideal standard-bearer in the world. The fate of the church is inextricably bound to the lives of the poor.

I am under no illusions that this is a far greater task than the one Scrooge faced. When given the opportunity to sift through a lifetime of selfishness and greed, Dickens's most famous character let the vision of an ugly end reinform and reinvigorate a vision of his future. Jesus has given us a vision of the kingdom of God, a vision of the end, of a future reality in which the *ptoxoi* are blessed to rule. Ours is the work of inauguration. But God is faithful, and it is clear that such an inauguration will contain both the bitterness of death and the promise of resurrection.

Bibliography

Arendt, Hannah. *The Origins of Totalitarianism*. London: Penguin Random House, 1951.

Aristotle. *Politics*. Translated by Benjamin Jowett. New York: Random House, 1943.

Bhatia, Aatish, et al. "Study of Elite College Admission Data Suggests Being Rich Is Its Own Qualification." *New York Times*, July 24, 2023. https://www.nytimes.com/interactive/2023/07/24/upshot/ivy-league-elite-college-admissions.html.

Biden, Joseph. "Full Transcript of President Biden's Farewell Address." *New York Times*, Jan. 15, 2025. https://www.nytimes.com/2025/01/15/us/politics/full-transcript-of-president-bidens-farewell-address.html.

Bornkamm, Günther. *Jesus of Nazareth*. Translated by Irene and Fraser McLuskey. New York: Harper & Row, 1960.

Boursier, Helen T. *Precious Precarity: A Spirituality of Borders*. Minneapolis: Fortress, 2024.

Boyle, Gregory. *Barking to the Choir: The Power of Radical Kinship*. New York: Simon & Schuster, 2017.

———. Foreword to *The Homeboy Way: A Radical Approach to Business and Life*, by Thomas Vozzo, vii–x. Chicago: Loyola, 2022.

———. *Tattoos on the Heart: The Power of Boundless Compassion*. New York: Free Press, 2010.

———. *The Whole Language: The Power of Extravagant Tenderness*. New York: Avid Reader, 2021.

Chetty, Raj, et al. "Diversifying Society's Leaders? The Determinants and Causal Effects of Admission to Highly Selective Private Colleges." NBER Working Paper Series 31492, National Bureau of Economic Research, rev. Oct. 2023. https://www.nber.org/papers/w31492.

Christopher, J. Clif. *Not Your Parents' Offering Plate: A New Vision for Financial Stewardship*. 2nd ed. Nashville: Abingdon, 2008. Kindle.

Coffin, William Sloane. *A Passion for the Possible: A Message to U.S. Churches*. Louisville: Westminster John Knox, 1993.

Commission for Racial Justice. *Toxic Wastes and Race in the United States: A National Report on the Racial and Socio-Economic Characteristics of Communities with Hazardous Waste Sites*. New York: United Church of Christ, 1987. https://www.ucc.org/wp-content/uploads/2020/12/ToxicWastesRace.pdf.

Desmond, Matthew. *Poverty, by America*. New York: Crown, 2023.

Dickens, Charles. *A Christmas Carol*. London: Heinemann, 1906.

BIBLIOGRAPHY

Doctrine of Discovery Project. "What Is the Doctrine of Discovery?" https://doctrineofdiscovery.org/what-is-the-doctrine-of-discovery/.

Duncan, Mike. "Appendix 10—The Revolution Devours Its Children." *Revolutions* (podcast), season 11, episode 12. Dec. 4, 2022.

———. *The Storm Before the Storm: The Beginning of the End of the Roman Republic*. New York: PublicAffairs, 2017.

Edmonson, Catie. "House Elects Mike Johnson as Speaker, Embracing a Hard-Right Conservative." *New York Times*, Oct. 25, 2023. https://www.nytimes.com/2023/10/25/us/politics/house-republicans-speaker-vote-johnson.html.

Eklund, Rebekah. *The Beatitudes Through the Ages*. Grand Rapids: Eerdmans, 2021.

Evangelical Lutheran Church in America. *Evangelical Lutheran Worship*. Minneapolis: Augsburg Fortress, 2006.

Fouirnaies, Alexander. "Public Funding of US Elections." University of Chicago Center for Effective Government, Jan. 25, 2024. https://effectivegov.uchicago.edu/primers/public-funding-of-us-elections.

Freire, Paulo. *Pedagogy of the Oppressed*. Translated by Myra Bergman Ramos. New York: Bloomsbury, 2000.

Friedman, Edwin H. *A Failure of Nerve: Leadership in the Age of the Quick Fix*. New York: Seabury, 1999.

Friesen, Steven J. "Poverty in Pauline Studies: Beyond the So-Called New Consensus." *Journal for the Study of the New Testament* 26 (2004) 323–61. https://doi.org/10.1177/0142064X0402600304.

Garrick, David. "San Diego Elected Officials Have Gotten 5 Raises Since Voters Overhauled Their Pay. Here's What They Make, and How It Compares." *San Diego Union-Tribune*, June 2, 2023. https://www.sandiegouniontribune.com/2023/06/02/san-diego-elected-officials-have-gotten-5-raises-since-voters-overhauled-their-pay-heres-what-they-make-and-how-it-compares/.

González, Justo L. *Luke*. Belief: A Theological Commentary on the Bible. Louisville: Westminster John Knox, 2010.

———. *The Story Luke Tells: Luke's Unique Witness to the Gospel*. Grand Rapids: Eerdmans, 2015.

Gutiérrez, Gustavo. *A Theology of Liberation: History, Politics, and Salvation*. Translated and edited by Sister Caridad Inda and John Eagleson. Maryknoll, NY: Orbis, 1988.

Hector, Kevin W. *Christianity as a Way of Life: A Systematic Theology*. New Haven: Yale University Press, 2023.

Himmelstein, David U., et al. "Medical Bankruptcy: Still Common Despite the Affordable Care Act." *American Journal of Public Health* 109 (2019) 431–33. https://doi.org/10.2105/AJPH.2018.304901.

Homeboy Industries. "Fact Sheet." https://homeboyindustries.org/wp-content/uploads/2023/05/HBfactsheet_3.0_KB-update-1-1.pdf.

Hotchkiss, Dan. *Governance and Ministry: Rethinking Board Leadership*. 2nd ed. Lanham, MD: Rowman & Littlefield, 2016.

Joas, Hans. *Faith as an Option: Possible Futures for Christianity*. Translated by Alex Skinner. Stanford: Stanford University Press, 2014.

Kaldellis, Anthony. *The New Roman Empire: A History of Byzantium*. New York: Oxford University Press, 2024.

Kelly, Kate. "S.E.C. Inquiry Into Former Senator's Stock Sales Is Closed Without Charges." *New York Times*, Jan. 6, 2023. https://www.nytimes.com/2023/01/06/us/politics/burr-sec-inquiry-closed.html.

Kendi, Ibram X. *How to Be an Anti-Racist*. New York: One World, 2019.

Khan-Cullors, Patrisse, and Asha Bandele. *When They Call You a Terrorist: A Black Lives Matter Memoir*. New York: St. Martin's Griffin, 2017.

Kimmerer, Robin Wall. *The Serviceberry: Abundance and Reciprocity in the Natural World*. New York: Scribner, 2024.

King, Martin Luther, Jr. "11 Months Before His Assassination, MLK Talks 'New Phase' of Civil Rights Struggle." Interview by Sander Vanocur. NBC News, May 8, 1967. https://www.nbcnews.com/video/martin-luther-king-jr-speaks-with-nbc-news-11-months-before-assassination-1202163779741.

———. "Letter from a Birmingham Jail." In *Why We Can't Wait*, 85–112. New York: New American Library, 1963.

Kittel, Gerhard, and Gerhard Friedrich, eds. *Theological Dictionary of the New Testament*. Translated by Geoffrey W. Bromiley. 10 vols. Grand Rapids: Eerdmans, 1964–1976.

Krueger, Alyson. "The Church Fixer." *New York Times*, Jan. 4, 2025. https://www.nytimes.com/2025/01/04/business/church-turnaround-fundraising-outreach.html.

La Boétie, Étienne de. "The Discourse of Voluntary Servitude." In *The Politics of Obedience and Étienne de la Boétie*, translated by Paul Bonnefon, 109–50. Montreal: Black Rose, 2007.

Levine, Amy-Jill, and Ben Witherington III. *The Gospel of Luke*. New Cambridge Bible Commentary. Cambridge: Cambridge University Press, 2018.

Lindner, Cynthia G. *Varieties of Gifts: Multiplicity and the Well-Lived Pastoral Life*. Lanham, MD: Rowman & Littlefield, 2016.

Long, Thomas G. *Accompany Them with Singing: The Christian Funeral*. Louisville: Westminster John Knox, 2009.

Martin, Philip, dir. "Smoke and Mirrors." *The Crown* (TV series), episode 5, season 1. Written by Peter Morgan, produced by Sony Pictures Television and Left Bank Pictures. Nov. 4, 2016.

McCrummen, Stephanie. "The Army of God Comes Out of the Shadows." *Atlantic*, Jan. 9, 2025. https://www.theatlantic.com/magazine/archive/2025/02/new-apostolic-reformation-christian-movement-trump/681092/.

Niebuhr, Reinhold. *Moral Man and Immoral Society: A Study in Ethics and Politics*. Louisville: Westminster John Knox, 1960.

Paulsen, David. "Episcopal Church Completes Divestment from Fossil Fuel Industry." Episcopal News Service, Dec. 11, 2024. https://episcopalnewsservice.org/2024/12/11/episcopal-church-completes-divestment-from-fossil-fuel-industry/.

Plato. *Republic*. Translated by C. D. C. Reeve. Indianapolis: Hackett, 2004.

Rossing, Barbara R. *The Rapture Exposed: The Message of Hope in the Book of Revelation*. New York: Basic, 2007.

Slodysko, Brian. "Sen. Burr Under Investigation Again for Pandemic Stock Sales." Associated Press, Oct. 28, 2021. https://apnews.com/article/coronavirus-pandemic-donald-trump-business-health-richard-burr-8294ed00c4098b295f7c5b21eac4614b.

Stout, Jeffrey. *Blessed Are the Organized: Grassroots Democracy in America*. Princeton: Princeton University Press, 2010.

Swanson, Richard W. *Provoking the Gospel of Luke: A Storyteller's Commentary, Year C*. Cleveland: Pilgrim, 2007.

BIBLIOGRAPHY

Swenson, Rachel. "On Accompaniment." Living Lutheran, Feb. 21, 2014. https://www.livinglutheran.org/2014/02/accompaniment/.

Taylor, Charles. *A Secular Age*. Cambridge: Harvard University Press, 2007.

Theoharis, Liz, and Colleen Wessel-McCoy. "'More than Flinging a Coin': True Compassion as a Critique of Charity." Kairos Center for Religions, Rights & Social Justice, Feb. 23, 2017. https://kairoscenter.org/compassion-as-a-critique-of-charity/.

Thurman, Howard. *Jesus and the Disinherited*. Boston: Beacon, 1976.

Tickle, Phyllis. *The Great Emergence: How Christianity Is Changing and Why*. New York: Baker, 2012.

Tweedy, Jeff. *Let's Go (So We Can Get Back): A Memoir of Recording and Discording with Wilco, Etc*. New York: Penguin Random House, 2018.

Vena, Osvaldo. "Commentary on Matthew 5:1–12." Working Preacher, Nov. 5, 2023. https://www.workingpreacher.org/commentaries/revised-common-lectionary/all-saints-sunday/commentary-on-matthew-5-1-12-10.

Vozzo, Thomas. *The Homeboy Way: A Radical Approach to Business and Life*. Chicago: Loyola, 2022.

www.ingramcontent.com/pod-product-compliance
Lightning Source LLC
Chambersburg PA
CBHW050810160426
43192CB00010B/1704